HUNGRY SOULS
—HOLY—
COMPANIONS:

Mentoring a New Generation of Christians

PATRICIA HENDRICKS

MOREHOUSE PUBLISHING

HARRISBURG · NEW YORK

Morehouse Publishing, P.O. Box 1321, Harrisburg, PA 17105

Morehouse Publishing, 445 Fifth Avenue, New York, NY 10016

Morehouse Publishing is an imprint of Church Publishing Incorporated.

Cover photography by Stephanie Sholly

Cover design by Laurie Klein Westhafer

Interior design by Irene Zevgolis

Library of Congress Cataloging-in-Publication Data

Hendricks, Patricia.
Hungry souls, holy companions : mentoring a new generation of Christians / Patricia Hendricks.
     p. cm.
Includes bibliographical references.
ISBN-13: 978-0-8192-2196-4 (pbk.)
   1. Mentoring in church work. 2. Spiritual formation. 3. Discipling (Christianity) I. Title.
BV4408.5.H46 2006
259'.25—dc22
                          2006022315

Printed in the United States of America

06 07 08 09   10 9 8 7 6 5 4 3 2 1

DEDICATION

*A special thank you
to those who shared their stories with me
during the interview process
of this book project.*

CONTENTS

INTRODUCTION

A group of twentysomethings in a large church of four thousand members in Illinois obtains permission from their pastor to conduct their own service. The service is held on Sunday evening in a small, darkened room with a few lit candles. There is no leader. Instead, members of the group take turns reading short passages of scripture followed by periods of silence. Julie is a regular participant at this alternative service. Burned out on entertainment styles of worship, she desires to experience God, together with a few people, in a sacred, silent space.

Across the globe in Taizé, France, more than one hundred thousand young adults, representing eighty countries, make the pilgrimage to this small village each summer. These young people participate in bible study, experience international community, and talk with spiritual directors. They attend the daily Taizé-style worship, which consists of meditative singing, candlelight, and silence. Eric comes from England with the hope that he might discover a closer connection with God. Alison, also from England, feels that a "happy, clappy" style of worship doesn't suit her. She journeys to Taizé looking for a personal, private style of worship that will help her with her prayer.

In my work as executive director of Christos Center for Spiritual Formation in St. Paul, Minnesota, I've talked with people like Julie and

Eric and Alison. In recent years, people in their twenties have contacted our center asking about spiritual formation and spiritual disciplines. They've requested spiritual directors and asked to be admitted into our spiritual direction preparation program. Young seminary students have also applied to our programs, seeking a balance to the instruction they receive in their courses. Heather, a second-year seminary student, acknowledged a common desire among seminarians: "I want heart knowledge as well as head knowledge."

As the requests from young people grew more numerous, I decided to embark on a study of this phenomenon. I conducted extensive interviews of youth workers, youth pastors, spiritual directors who have young directees, campus ministers, and college spiritual formation directors. I interviewed youth and young adults—people whose ages ranged from 16 to 30. This book is the result of four years of research.

As I reflected on that research, I asked myself these questions: What is happening, spiritually, to today's young people? Are they pursuing a life of faith? How does their pursuit differ from that of previous generations? Are they open to receiving spiritual companionship from older adults? As I pondered the answers to these questions, insights began to surface and I realized that some young people are actively pursuing a faith life, while others are not. Some are asking serious God questions at the age of 18 and 26, while others start at a young age, drift away, and then come back. And there are those who may never feel the need to pursue a faith walk.

As I further reflected on my research, I was surprised at the hunger young people have for spiritual growth. I became convinced that the call to respond to the restlessness in our hearts for God is for all ages. In short, I learned never to assume that people are too young to understand spiritual depth. A confirmation class of 15- and 16-year-olds responded to this question: Where did you notice God in worship today? "I saw God in the light shining through the stained-glass window." "I saw God in my grandfather's eyes as we passed the sign of peace." "I felt God's presence in the candlelight." As their confirmation mentor listened to the answers, she observed, "Kids are profoundly aware of their spirituality if they are given the chance."

This book is about those in their teens and twenties who are seeking spiritual growth and for the adults who walk with those youthful seekers—spiritual directors, parish workers, campus ministers, parents, and teachers. As I conducted my interviews, what often surfaced was a desire for adult companionship. Young people need authentic and committed companions who can invite them to question and to seek and who can affirm the yearnings of their hearts. It's normal for today's young people to seek companionship among their peers. They are comfortable with community. Many were nurtured in day-care centers and preschools, and they rely on that network into their young adulthood. Like the cast of the television series *Friends*, they gather at coffee shops, restaurants, street corners, homes, and apartments to discuss their problems and opinions. When they're not actually with people, they're on cell phones, or they're e-mailing or instant messaging.

But when I asked young people about the quality of advice they receive from their peers, most of those in their twenties agreed with Anna, 24: "My peers are just as clueless as I am." Today's youth want relationships with older adults—people who have been through some of the difficulties of life—people who are "less clueless."

I use the word "youth" to refer to adolescents, those between the ages of 13 and 19. Young adult refers to people in their twenties. Young people and youthful seekers refer to the combined groups of youth and young adults.

Spiritual director and youth leader Mark Gardner agrees. "Today's young adults are fragile," he says. "They don't want to be won over to the faith by glitzy programs and big concerts. They want to know if anyone will be there for them over the long haul. They want to know if anyone will look at their cracked lives and think, 'I like you. I'll be here for you.' They want to know if others feel as broken as they do. They want to know if they can trust you with their secrets. They want to know if you're broken, too, and how you are putting yourself back together." This book is intended for those of you in the "trenches" with people of the younger generations: spiritual directors, youth pastors, lay youth workers, campus ministers, teachers, parents, and college spiritual formation directors. And it's for those of you in your teens and twenties—whether you work with youth or are trying to find your own place in the milieu of religious belief.

This book is a smorgasbord of ideas, stories, experiences, and practical suggestions on how to companion youthful seekers. I invite you to treat it as a smorgasbord, and pick and choose among the assortment. Allow ideas to stimulate your creativity and your passion. Not all the suggestions will work with your particular group or in your setting, so sift through them as if you were panning for gold, and find what works for you. Experiment; play with the ideas. Most importantly, pause frequently as you read and listen to what God's spirit is teaching you. Then pray for the grace and courage to act on that guidance.

There's something unique about this wave of kids. They want more depth, and they need people who can help them find that depth. They need someone older than themselves.

–Susan Groah, spiritual director and youth leader

---------------------- CHAPTER ONE ----------------------

HUNGRY SOULS: WHO ARE THEY?

ERIC, JEREMY, NICOLE, ALICIA

Eric, 26, was raised Lutheran. He attended a Baptist youth group during his high school years, and in college he left the institutional church but often discussed religion with classmates. He's married to a woman who was raised in the Episcopal Church, and lately they've been looking for a new church home. They visit various churches searching for one that feels comfortable. Denominational affiliation is of lesser importance than a feeling of welcome.

Jeremy, 28, considers himself independent of organized religion. He went to a Methodist church as a child because his parents insisted. Now, he believes there is some truth in all religions. He has used the Internet to research different beliefs, and he takes ideas from the Buddhist, Christian, and Jewish traditions. As he participates in chat rooms with others who like to discuss religion, he feels he'll never join a specific church because it would be too limiting.

Nicole, 29, left the Catholic Church after she graduated from high school. She's come to spiritual direction because she feels an emptiness, "like something is missing in my life." But she feels she can't go back to the faith of her parents. She doesn't want to be told what to believe; nor does she want a religion that "comes in a package of do's and don'ts."

Alicia, 17, belongs to the Episcopal Church where she was baptized. She sees no need to look further. She's happy there. Her friends are there, and the youth group "rocks." She feels respected by the clergy and the older members of the church. She served on the liturgy committee and has preached on Sunday morning with other members of Journey into Adulthood class.

A PARADIGM SHIFT TO POSTMODERNISM

If you're over 40, you realize these anecdotes illustrate dramatic shifts in the ways people practice their Christian faith today. Denominational loyalty among the young is rare. In fact, this era is often called the post-denominational era. Today's seekers have the freedom to question. They have instant access to information on world religions and the means to shop around for their religious beliefs.

It's an understatement to say that today's youth believe differently than other generations of youth. Today's young people were raised in a transitional society that moved from modern philosophy (scientific, rational, compartmentalized) to a postmodern one (technological, communal, holistic). People raised in the postmodern era have a different worldview than those raised under the influence of modern philosophy.

The postmodern philosophical shift started to take root in the mid-twentieth century, as Western society shifted from the industrial era to the information age, and as society began to see that science didn't have all the answers. As Western society entered the new millennium, the transition from modernism to postmodernism was nearly complete.

Postmodernism differs from modernism in many ways. Modern philosophy relies on reason, science and intellect. While postmodern ways of thinking don't discount reason, the elements of emotion, intuition, and subjective thinking are added to the philosophical mix. Generally speaking, modernism relies on rational thought and observation to obtain truth and often dismisses the spiritual aspects of humankind. Postmodernism admits that there are other ways to obtain truth such as experience, emotions, intuition, and a connection with the Divine. The postmodern thinker is more open to learning about religion through stories and experience than through theological constructs.

A modern thinker is comfortable with hierarchy and central authority. A postmodern thinker prefers individual or communal interpretation of experience, and is skeptical of authority. Finally, postmodernism is more inclusive and tolerant of diversity than is modernism.

Author Tony Jones, in *Postmodern Youth Ministry*, summarizes the differences between the two philosophies:

Modern Value	Postmodern Value
Rational	Experiential
Scientific	Spiritual
Unanimity (Homogeneous)	Pluralistic
Exclusive	Relative
Egocentric	Altruistic
Individualistic	Communal, Relational
Functional	Creative
Industrial	Environmental
Local Focus	Global Focus
Compartmentalized	Holistic
Relevant	Authentic[1]

POSTMODERNISM AND TODAY'S YOUNG BELIEVERS

Most of today's teens and twentysomethings were raised at the end of the transition from the modern era to the postmodern one. What are these young postmoderns looking for in the Christian church, and what do they desire for their own personal faith? Leonard Sweet, who writes about the postmodern church, uses the acronym EPIC (Experience, Participation, Image, Connection) to describe the spiritual search of today's young people.

EXPERIENTIAL FAITH

Today's postmodern believers would rather experience spiritual truths than read about them. "I want to experience my Creator now," says Erin, a 32-year-old Lutheran pastor working in her first church. Far from being "armchair Christians," today's youth aren't satisfied to sit in the pew and watch. They want to feel God's presence and are open to different ways to experience the Divine.

Today's opportunities for experiential faith range from Christian rock, to megachurch-style worship with lively choirs and full orchestras, to the quiet of more meditative types of worship. In fact, new seekers are becoming more open to the experience of quiet and ancient ritual. They are drawn to pre-Reformation styles of prayer, which invite a deeper awareness of God's presence.

Many of today's teens and twentysomethings are no longer engaged when church services become too casual, too MTV. They're pulled in a new direction. "Anything that seems old-fashioned, that's where they're going," says youth minister Mary Pat Tlingman. They're drawn to such complex ancient rituals as the Jewish Kabbalah, the walk of the labyrinth, the meditations of St. Ignatius, or the mantra-like recitations of Taizé.[2]

> *This is really a moment in the culture where many are attracted to silence, solitude, and mystery, and that can be across political spectrums from fundamentalist to extremely liberal, because those experiences of silence, mystery and solitude hold out the hope of being in touch with something more permanent.*
>
> —Tom Beaudoin, *Virtual Faith*

The experience of silence provides an atmosphere for young people that differs from their noisy, often chaotic life, and it is this difference, this quiet, that gives them a sense of God's presence. "I go to the dance club on Saturday night where I'm surrounded by loud music and people," says Tony, 27. "On Sunday morning, I want to encounter God in the quiet—quiet music, quiet prayers, time to think and not be distracted by noise."

THE EXPERIENCE OF MYSTERY

Along with the desire to experience God, this new generation of Christians is comfortable with mystery. Today's youthful seekers don't need to have everything explained to them. A number of years ago, I had the privilege of hearing Leonard Sweet conduct a seminar on postmodern thought where he used his acronym "EPIC." One of his statements impressed me as a core truth about today's younger generations: "Postmoderns don't approach life as a problem to be solved but a mystery to be experienced and lived."

Tom Beaudoin, Roman Catholic theologian and author of *Virtual Faith: The Irreverent Spiritual Quest of Generation X*, says: "There is room for mystery. In fact in their faith walk, today's youth often welcome mystery and sometimes are drawn to the mystical traditions of the Christian church. Meditative prayer, silence, ritual, and pilgrimage draw today's youth."[3]

Colleen Carroll, in *The New Faithful*, shares some key elements that many young believers are seeking:

- Their identity is centered on their religious beliefs, and their morality derives from those beliefs.
- They yearn for mystery and tend to trust their intuitive sense that what they have found is true, real, and worth living to the extreme.
- They seek guidance and formation from legitimate sources of authority. . . .
- They strive for personal holiness, authenticity and integration in their spiritual lives and are attracted to people and congregations that do the same.[4]

THE EXPERIENCE OF SACRED SPACE

If we combine a hunger for the experience of God with a yearning for mystery and a comfort with the transcendent, we understand why today's youthful seekers could potentially be drawn to churches that feel holy. The sacred space, and the combination of story and sacrament, of the more liturgical churches are very appealing to some. The ritual of the Episcopalian, Roman Catholic, Lutheran, and Eastern Orthodox churches are becoming attractive to the younger generations. Tony Jones comments, "When you walk into an Orthodox sanctuary, you

> *Christians are sitting on the most rich, elaborate, and beautiful symbolic language in God's creation, but we seem afraid to teach it to our young people. Every element of the liturgy has meaning. . . . Everything the priest wears symbolizes something . . . every word spoken from a prayer book or hymnal or the Bible has rich history. And postmodern students want to know these symbols—they want to touch the past.*
>
> *—Tony Jones, Postmodern Youth Ministry*

walk into another universe—and this makes sense to the postmodern mind: if there is a God, surely he dwells in a different place and space than we do. . . . Thus a high church sanctuary offers smells and bells worship that transports the communicant to another realm. This is done through incense, music, lighting, architecture and even kneeling in worship."[5]

Let's look again at the story of the group of twentysomethings in a large megachurch who were weary of entertainment-style worship and who opted to worship in silence. Like this group, many—of course not all—of today's faith seekers desire something different, something that transcends the ordinary. They're seeking someone bigger, someone they can't put into a box. They want to experience that kind of God.

I issue a challenge to those in the Episcopal, Lutheran, Roman Catholic, and Orthodox churches to prepare to welcome a new generation of people seeking faith through sacred and experiential ritual. But I add a caution. Today's young people welcome a return to the ancient faith practices which lead to a deep relationship with God. But, they will reject the ancient attitudes of rigidity, law, and judgment.

PARTICIPATORY FAITH

Many of today's young Christians want to take an active role in their faith walk, and I like to refer to them as "non-armchair seekers." They're open to traveling thousands of miles to go on a pilgrimage. They walk the maze-like path of the labyrinth. They participate in social justice activities, volunteering for Habitat for Humanity or going on mission trips in their own countries or to other parts of the world. These young people want to practice their Christian faith by serving others. Not yet having accumulated wealth, these seekers are willing and eager to give their time and energy. In fact, volunteerism is on the rise among today's youth. A 2005 *USA Weekend* survey of youth and volunteerism revealed a Millennial generation with a growing reputation for service: "A higher share of high school students

The labyrinth is an ancient Christian practice of "virtual pilgrimage" through walking a maze-like circle that leads to a center. It enables people to clear their minds of concerns and to open themselves to God's presence and guidance.

are community volunteers today [more than 65%] than ever before measured, going back half a century."[6]

Often this participatory faith allows the young person to see God in different situations. Brian, 16, spoke before his parish after a mission trip to Tennessee. "I felt God there in a different way than I feel God here in church. I felt God being proud of me as I scraped and painted houses."

Those who belong to a church want to participate in the mission of that church. They want a voice and desire to be heard and respected. Heather and Alison, both 17, volunteer in their Catholic parish during the weekly twenty-four-hour devotion before the Blessed Sacrament. They opt for the 1:00–2:00 a.m. shift because, as they explain, "We're up anyway. Everyone knows that teenagers don't go to bed until 3:00 a.m. This way the older people of the parish can sleep."

IMAGE-BASED FAITH

Raised with television, film, video games, VCRs, and the Internet, this new generation of Christians is visually stimulated. Generally speaking, young adults believe that film, more than television, portrays deep insights into life. Film presents traditional myths such as good versus evil, a hero's journey, companionship along the journey, and a hero's sacrifice—consider *The Lord of the Rings*, the Harry Potter films, and *The Lion, the Witch, and the Wardrobe*. Film depicts historical stories of exceptional bravery, loyalty, and love, and affirms the mentor/learner role and the master/student relationship: Yoda and Luke Skywalker, Harry Potter and Professor Dumbledore, Frodo and Gandalf.

Images of films stay with people and often contribute to their personal belief system. Spiritual director and coordinator of the summer internship program, Mary Martin-Wiens of Christ Presbyterian Church near Minneapolis calls this phenomenon "film iconography"—images captured in film that symbolize basic human truths or capture images of God. Images, therefore, are the common language of today's youthful seekers, and they reference lines of a film or a song in their conversations. I once overheard a conversation between two 18-year-old girls. One was describing a particular romantic moment with her boyfriend as a "you complete me" moment—a pivotal line from the film *Jerry Maguire*.

Rick, a youth leader in a rural Lutheran church, understands the role image plays with his high school students. He uses images and atmosphere in the prayer experience he conducts for them in a small chapel. As they arrive for youth group, they're instructed not to enter the chapel until they're ready. Inside, they take off their shoes to honor the holy ground, and they maintain silence. They sit on the floor around a center table. On the table are candles and an icon, a cross, or a clay form. Slowly, one by one, each person lights a candle. The image of the lit candles keeps the group focused. When each has lit a candle, a member of the group reads a short passage of scripture, and they are silent once again. The service ends with prayer petitions and a song.

CONNECTIVE-BASED FAITH

Once today's seekers experience the transcendent, they're eager to share that experience with others. A postmodern quality prevalent with today's youth is connection with others. While the previous baby boomer generation valued individuality, today's younger generation values community. "My generation values mystery, inclusion of all kinds of people, volunteerism, and intuitive ways of knowing," says Mary Martin-Wiens, 30. "Community is one of the two paramount thirsts of our souls. The other thirst is for the real."

Compared to past generations, today's young adults grew up with fewer adults in their lives. Many were moved away from extended family and raised in day-care centers until they became latchkey kids. Nurtured with peers in a communal setting, they rely on that network into their young adulthood. They like to talk about their experiences, and telling stories is a favorite means of communication. After walking the labyrinth for the first time, at an Episcopal church in Minneapolis, these young adults had this to say to their adult advisor:

MIKE, 16: I felt like I was close to God and I could relax and not get lost.

HEIDI, 18: The labyrinth helped me to realize that the path through life isn't easy and there are many twists and turns. But it showed me that even if you get off the path, God is always with you to get you back on.

JENNIFER, 16: Very peaceful, felt like a big hug.

After walking the labyrinth, Jennifer, Heidi, and Mike were eager to share their experiences with their adult leader. This generation of young people yearns to be listened to—both by their peers and by older adults. "These folks are hungry for someone to genuinely listen to them and help them discern who God has called them to be," says Emily, a spiritual director to young adults in northern California. But there are "strings" attached to this hunger. The people in this generation value authenticity and nonjudgmentalism. They simply want to know if you care enough about them to listen to their stories and to be committed to them.

BEYOND EPIC

Today's youth are seeking a faith that welcomes participation, offers images, and encourages connection; moreover, this generation values inclusiveness in relationships and ideas. They are generally accepting of others' beliefs, and they often have a subjective outlook on life. Truth is perceived as personal and relative, and they find it difficult to stand outside a situation and judge it. One reason for this inclusive and subjective outlook is their connection with the global community. Many of today's young people have the funds and the opportunity to visit and to study in other countries, where they meet people of cultures who have different histories, and practice different faiths. Some of today's youth travel, not physically but virtually, by surfing the Internet. They communicate with Russians, South Africans, and Indonesians, exchanging ideas, opinions, and stories. Moreover, they're being raised in a society that's no longer exclusively Judeo-Christian. Recent immigration trends have resulted in a diversity of people settling in the United States, Canada, and Western Europe. Today's youth have classmates, neighbors, friends, relatives, and coworkers of many racial and ethnic backgrounds.

Finally, many of today's youth are seeking authenticity in faith. Several college-age students expressed to me a distinction between being a "trendy" Christian and being an authentic Christian, citing several examples in today's popular culture of the exploitation of Christianity through fashion, jewelry, music, books, film, and television. These college students want to practice an authentic faith—a faith that teaches them how to live their lives as Christ lived. It's no wonder that many of these young people are drawn to ancient traditions of prayer and ritual. The practices feel authentic to them.

With the globe at their fingertips through vast pools of information, today's youth have choices—and they have power. They no longer need to go through adults to obtain information. They have ready access to the Internet, and they use this access to learn about the options available to today's Christians. Recent studies have indicated that today's teens and twentysomethings spend more time on the computer than watching television. At their fingertips are vast sources of information on the background of different faith practices and on how belief in God has evolved throughout history—and they're eager to apply that information to their own growing faith. Today's young Christians want meat and not fluff from the information highway, and they ask themselves this question: "How does this information relate to my search for God?"

TAIZÉ, FRANCE: A MICROCOSM OF TODAY'S SEEKERS

Today's young people are globally connected. They hunger for information and connection with others. They respond to experiences and are comfortable with mystery. It's no wonder that young people from around the world journey to the village of Taizé, France. There they spend a week studying the Bible, praying, singing, participating in spiritual direction, and visiting with people of other nations. There's no other place in the world like it.

The ministry of Taizé began in 1940 by a Christian brother from Switzerland who felt a call to create a community where simplicity and kindheartedness would be lived. Brother Roger settled in Taizé, France, and invited his sister Genevieve to come and help with hospitality.

During World War II, Taizé became a safe place for refugees fleeing the war. Many of the refugees were Jewish, so Brother Roger went off into the woods to pray alone so that non-Christians would not feel threatened. After the war, Taizé became an orphanage for boys left homeless by the war.

By the end of the 1950s, young adults between the ages of 17 and 30 began coming to Taizé, drawn by the style of prayer, song, and international community. Today, young adults from seventy-five countries arrive every week from early spring to late autumn. During some of the summer months, as many as five thousand young people visit each week. They're cared for by the brothers, who now comprise a community of Roman Catholic and Protestant men, as well as two orders of Catholic sisters.

Why do so many young people travel thousands of miles to pilgrimage there? For what are they searching? Let's allow the young pilgrims to tell the story:

What has Taizé been for me? It was a place of simplicity and silence where I could seek God. It was a place where people my age came from all over the world, and together we lived a life closer to God. The superficial trappings of the world fell away. Humbly and so quietly the brothers created a place where thousands of young people can see the Lord. Seeking and searching are encouraged. I wasn't given a single answer at Taizé. I was only given time and space to listen to God."
–Sarah, undergraduate, Wake Forest University

As a student at Wake Forest, my life is full of instant gratification and constant activity. For me, Taizé was a place to become reacquainted with my true self in the eyes of God—to hear the still small voice of my soul . . . Taizé is a place of acceptance. In the monastery each individual is loved for who they really are. Everyone feels comfortable and even secure in removing the masks they so often wear. Taizé is a place of rediscovery.
–Ashleigh, undergraduate, Wake Forest University

I've never been able to sit still and appreciate silence. I've always been extrovert. But I found faith and love and

> *calmness from inside myself rather than from other people . . .*
> *I've found an inner peace within me."*
> —Tim, England
>
> Pilgrims to Taizé have the option of meeting with adults to
> process their experiences through a spiritual direction ministry
> provided by the Sisters of the Community of St. Andrew. "We're
> listening to these young people in a way that lets each person
> know that she is loved by God," says Sister Barbara. "What
> allows us to do this is the trust that God is there for both of us.
> We're both searching for God. One person may have a little
> more experience than the other and can help the young person
> recognize what her true freedom is."

Taizé, France, is a place that represents a growing trend among young
Christians today. Mary Martin-Wiens, summarizes this trend: "The kind
of Christianity that will attract the new generation will be authentic,
inclusive, comfortable with diversity, more open to a dynamic growing
faith than a static, fixed system, more visual than verbal, and with a high
level of tolerance and ambiguity. There will be room for experience,
mysticism, and mystery."

It's important to note that the qualities mentioned in this chapter
don't include all people under the age of 30. Today's youth have the
freedom to pick and choose which postmodern trends and which
spiritual practices to follow. It is also true that people in midlife and
older can be postmodern in their thinking. What's important for the
spiritual companion to know is that all age groups are affected by this
new philosophy: young people, middle-aged folks, as well as the parents
and grandparents of youth.

THE SHIFT IN GENERATIONS

Along with a philosophical paradigm shift from modernism to postmodernism, there's a generational shift happening with today's people in
their teens and twenties. According to recent literature, today's teens and
twentysomethings come from two generations: Generation X and the

Millennial generation. The Gen Xers were born between 1961 and 1981; the Millennials, between 1982 and 2002. In fact, as this book goes to press in 2006, today's late-twentysomethings are the tail end of the X Generation. Knowledge of each generation can shed some light on the emotional and spiritual makeup of these young people.

GENERATION X

Born between 1961 and 1981, this generation is smaller in number (51 million), sandwiched between two generational dynasties: the baby boomers, 76 million strong, and the Millennials, numbering 73 million. Considered by many as the generation that had the least adult involvement in their early years, they were the first generation of children of widespread divorce and two-income families. They were the first "latchkey" kids who came home from school to an empty house and a television. Many members of this generation report spending more time with television than with their parents during childhood. Because of their lack of adult involvement, this group is both self-reliant and communal. At an early age, they learned to rely on their peers for support and are fiercely loyal to their friends.

Members of this generation were infants and children when the United States went through the disillusioned period of the 1970s. Some were schoolchildren during the Watergate scandal and the Iran hostage crisis. Many sat in their schoolrooms on January 28, 1986, and witnessed the tragic explosion of the Challenger spacecraft. They're a skeptical generation with little confidence in institutions and authority, and this skepticism surrounds their religious views. This generation claims to be spiritual but not religious, finding God outside of church—in the popular culture of music, film, and music video. But I've found that as this generation ages, they're beginning the journey back to the traditions of the institutional churches, especially if the particular church is willing to welcome and empower them.

The Generation Xers were the last generation to have an inkling of the industrial era and were raised in the era of the blossoming information age—the age of new technology, which included video games (Pong, Pac-man, Donkey Kong, Gauntlet), video arcades, hand-held electronic games, miniature calculators, boom boxes, cable TV, MTV, the remote, and the birth of the personal computer. In addition, this generation had more disposable income than previous generations—money to spend on the new forms of entertainment.

MILLENNIAL GENERATION

Born between 1982 and 2002, this generation only knows the age of technology. They've always known life with a remote, a microwave, video games, answering machine, computer, and a VCR. According to Rick Hicks and Kathy Hicks, authors of *Boomers, Xers, and Other Strangers*, "They have never used a rotary dial phone. They have always cooked popcorn in a microwave. The *Tonight Show* has always been with Jay Leno. Atari predates them, as do vinyl record albums."[7] This is the first generation that knows more than its elders (about technology, that is), and the first generation that doesn't need authority figures to help them access information—many were surfing the Internet before they were allowed to cross the street alone. This generation is being raised with many adults in their lives: parents, teachers, coaches, mentors, and church workers; in general, they respect their elders. They were born in an era in which children were wanted—the "it takes a village to raise a child" era. Legislation such as No Child Left Behind is being implemented to assure that this generation of youth has opportunities. Generally speaking, they're more positive, more achievement oriented, more cooperative than previous generations—and they're more desirous of having older adults act as mentors.

Each generation learns from the previous one, and the Millennials are carrying a few Gen X qualities with them as they become adults. The sense of community is strong with the Millennials; they also demonstrate a general restlessness around religion, and many in the Millennial generation are looking to reclaim the significance of religious tradition just as some Gen Xers are doing. Like the members of Generation X, Millenials are susceptible to popular culture, and they have money to spend on the merchandise of that culture.

While the Gen Xers *accept* diversity among peoples, the Millennial generation *celebrates* diversity. William Strauss and Neil Howe, writers on the topic of generational differences, explain the demographics of the new generation as the most racially and ethnically diverse and least

Caucasian group of young adults. They cite one revealing U.S. statistic: "In 1999, nonwhites and Latinos accounted for nearly 36 percent of the 18 or under population."[8]

Baby Boomers: The Prequel

The adults who will companion the new generations of seekers in most cases will come from the baby boomer generation. Born between 1945 and 1960, in many respects, this generation set a tone for the two generations to follow. The boomers were the first generation to question, in large numbers, institutional religion, and to be ecumenical in their searching. Because they were the first generation after WWII, and because there were so many of them, they became a focal point for the culture. They were carefully nurtured as children and were given many more educational opportunities than previous generations. They were an optimistic generation, certain that the future belonged to them, and they were a serious and philosophical generation who questioned authority and the norms of society. Often this philosophical thinking led them to rebellion. At a young age, members of this generation marched for civil rights, protested the war in Vietnam, questioned their beliefs in God, and left the institutional church in droves. While they are often considered self-centered and materialistic, they're also compassionate. Many served in the inner city, worked as advocates for the disabled, and volunteered for the Peace Corps.

In many respects, there are parallels between the boomer generation and today's Millennial generation. Maybe that's why it's natural for one to serve as mentor to the other. Like the boomers, today's Millennials are serious about life. They ponder, question, and act on their observations. They're well-educated and positive about the future. While it's a little early to tell, they may not be as materialistic as the boomers. Many have a desire to serve the poor and disadvantaged of the world, and they're going on mission trips in droves.

Recently I spent some time with International Teams, headquartered in Elgin, Illinois. The organization trains missionaries for work in Europe, the United States, South America, and Asia. Sarah Anderson, director of learning and training, reports that generally two groups engage in missionary work—those in their twenties and those in their fifties and early sixties. Maybe there's a synergy between the boomers and the Millennials. Only the passing of the years will tell.

YOUTH AND POPULAR CULTURE

A chapter on today's youthful seekers isn't complete without a few words about popular culture, which includes music, film, television, MTV, news media, advertising, video games, computer games, the Internet (advertising, gaming, communication, and information), sports (both spectator and participatory), fashion (clothing, jewelry, makeup, and body art), books, magazines, newspapers, comic books, pop art, toys, and hobbies. Popular culture is driven by the advertising and entertainment industries, and its influence is immeasurable. It seeps into our very bones. Nor can any of us, young or old, completely comprehend the influence today's culture has on our spiritual belief systems.

Those who mentor today's young people don't need to know everything about the film, video games, and music of today's youth culture; nor do they need to like today's modes of entertainment. Young people don't expect that. They expect older adults to "act their age" and to be authentic. What youth workers need to know is that pop culture is the fabric of what today's youth are about. The two cannot be separated. However, many people who companion young believers do enjoy some of today's entertainment. Through my interviewing process, I noted that both young and older adults enjoy conversations about film. Film appeals to today's love of image. The cinematography, the acting, and the music awaken the emotions. Because film is iconographic, with mythical themes of good and evil and heroism, it can provide unlimited opportunities for discussion.

STAR WARS, A POP CULTURE PHENOMENON

The best example of film influencing popular culture is the Star Wars phenomenon. From its first release in 1977 to its most recent episode in 2005, this film franchise has had a major impact on film, video games, fiction, toys, and even spirituality. Mythical themes such as good and evil, a hero's journey, sacrifice, and the master/apprentice relationship are major elements of the Star Wars films. Who can forget the many images of good and evil: Luke and Darth Vader, Luke and Jabba; Anakin and the dark side. Who can forget the intergalactic journeys of the series' heroes or the sacrifices of key characters? Who doesn't recall the image of Yoda mentoring young Luke in the ancient ways of the force? And how many times have we thought about the words, "May the force be with you?"

Star Wars images are as much a part of many people's spiritual awareness as are some of the images from the scriptures. Today's young people literally grew up in the Star Wars era, surrounded by the films, the toys, the characters, and the theology. Is it possible that today's interest in ancient traditions is driven by Luke's hunger for the ancient power of the Jedi Knights? In an interview with Bill Moyers, Star Wars creator George Lucas said, "I would hesitate to call the Force God. It is designed primarily to make young people think about mystery. Not to say 'Here's the answer.' It is to say, Think about this for a second. Is there a God? What does God look like? What does God sound like? What does God feel like? How do we relate to God?' Just getting young people to think at that level is what I've been trying to do in the films."[9]

NAVIGATING IN THE WORLD OF POPULAR CULTURE

It's impossible to keep up with the trends in popular culture. The best advice I can give to those who companion youth is simply to be aware that all of us are influenced by pop culture—more than we imagine. Young people talk about the film and the music of today, and we can

It is impossible for any one individual to keep up with the changing trends of popular culture. I recommend a Web page that stays current with the trends, especially in film and music: www.explorefaith.com.

listen. If a young person refers to a song, a television show, a film that you know nothing about, ask. Most young people delight in explaining a film to us older folks. Moreover, they like to be asked probing questions: What does this song/film say to you? What was the main message you receive through this work? How does the film/song teach you more about human nature? What does it say about good and evil? What does the film/song say about God? What are you noticing in the music you listen to or the films you watch that make you think or question?

WRAP-UP

In 1998, Tom Beaudoin published *Virtual Faith*, the first book to focus on the religious experience of Generation X and the first book to address the effect of popular culture on faith. Since then, books as well as web pages, explain popular culture, the generations, postmodernism, today's Christian climate, and youth ministry.

The sources I've read and the people I've interviewed agree on one truth: Today's young people are looking for something meaningful in their lives and something authentic for their religious beliefs. My hope as I write this book is that we Christians who have been around for a time will provide guidance for these young people. If we don't attend to the hunger of these youthful seekers, society could lose a talented and vital generation of Christian believers.

NOTES

1. Tony Jones, *Postmodern Youth Ministry: Exploring Cultural Shift, Creating Holistic Connections, Cultivating Authentic Community* (Grand Rapids, MI: Youth Specialities/Zondervan Publishing, 2001), 30–37.

2. Neil Howe and William Strauss, *New Millennia's Rising: The Next Great Generation,* (New York: Vintage Books, 2000), 236.

3. Tom Beaudoin, *Virtual Faith, The Irreverent Spiritual Quest of Generation X* (San Francisco: Jossey-Bass, 1998), 164.

4. Colleen Carroll, *The New Faithful, Why Young Adults Are Embracing Christian Orthodoxy* (Chicago: Loyola Press, 2002), 15.

5. Tony Jones, *Postmodern Youth Ministry,* 97.

6. *USA Weekend,* June 2005, 6.

7. Rick Hicks and Kathy Hicks, *Boomers, Xers, and Other Strangers: Understanding the Generational Differences that Divide Us.* (Carol Stream, IL: Tyndale, 1999), 267–68.

8. Neil Howe and William Strauss, *Millennials Rising: The Next Great Generation,* 15.

9. See www.explorefaith.com/news.

—————————— CHAPTER TWO ——————————

ISSUES FACING YOUTHFUL SEEKERS: RELATIONSHIPS/VOCATION/ IDENTITY/FAITH

As with previous generations, today's youth have grave concerns and probing questions, from the personal to the global. Episcopal priest Susan Astarita of the University of Maryland says that today's college students are "beginning to realize that there are grand questions for which the secular life can't provide answers. . . . These students are people who did not grow up with a strict value system, and now they are asking perplexing questions."[1]

So how *did* today's youth grow up, and with what kind of value system? "Deconstructed" is one term that describes the society from which today's youth emerged. In *Reconstructing Catholicism for a New Generation*, Robert Ludwig explains the phenomenon this way: "The breakup of family structure, business and political scandals, the material-istic ambiance of ubiquitous TV commercials and suburban shopping malls . . . the rapid growth of theft and violent crime—all are sympto-matic of the deconstructed world, which is the only world today's young people have ever known."[2]

Youth pastor Steve Wiens of Christ Presbyterian Church in Minneapolis, uses another word to describe the society that nurtured today's youth—fragmented. He cites fast-paced lives and fragmented families as two major issues for today's young people. "One of the common questions that I typically ask teenagers when I meet them is if they live with both of their parents," he explains. "It is not a secret that almost 60 percent of marriages end in divorce, so statistically speaking, most of the teenagers that I work with come from a family unit that does not include both a mother and a father." The typical teenager today juggles full-time school, a part-time job, and extracurricular activities such as sports, drama, and church, plus a full schedule of activities with their friends.

Fragmentation and deconstruction plus the complexity of today's life and culture compose the background material from which questions and issues emerge for today's young people. As they transition into adulthood, they experience a quarterlife crisis, a term coined by Alexandra Robbins and Abby Wilner, coauthors of *Quarterlife Crisis: The Unique Challenges of Life in Your Twenties*. They say, "The transition from childhood to adulthood—from school to the world beyond—comes as a jolt for which many of today's twentysomethings simply are not prepared. The resulting overwhelming senses of helplessness and cluelessness, of indecision and apprehension, make up the real and common experience we call the quarterlife crisis."[3]

This crisis can last for several years. In fact, social scientists are beginning to talk about a longer time of transition between childhood and adulthood. People in their twenties are delaying marriage, education, and career choice, creating a new stage that can last from the age of 18 to 25 or even longer. New names for young adults in this in-between stage are beginning to appear in our language: "twixters," "youthhood," and "thresholders."

One of the major roles of adult mentors is to model healthy adult behavior to those "thresholders" and to listen to their questions and address their issues. Those issues fall into four categories: relationships, vocation, personal identity, and faith.

THE CRISIS OF RELATIONSHIPS

Am I lovable?
Do I want partnership or marriage?
Will I ever be sure enough about someone to marry?
Is the person I am now with the one I want to be with for a

long time?
Will I ever be able to be friends with my parents?
Can I find someone I can talk to?
Why don't my friends seem to like me?
How can I cope with this breakup?[4]

Relationships among youth are varied and complex, running the gamut from family and peer relationships to institutional relationships involving school, team, job, or church. Young adults traditionally leave the security of family, and issues during this time include stretching the limits of accountability to parents and coping with living away from home. This is a time when an older adult mentor can assist a young person in bridging the gap between family dependence and autonomy. Young adults are freer to tell a mentor or spiritual director more than they would say to a family member or to a peer. A college student confided in her spiritual director, "I can't talk to my friends about this. They couldn't advise me, but my mom just found out she has cancer, and I don't know how to help her."

Many relationship issues involve peers. Dating, sexual intimacy, and the loss of friends are of immense concern simply because peer relationships are vital to today's young people. One issue that surfaced among many of the people I interviewed was the loss of friends, which happens during two key times of a young adult's life: after high school and after completing postsecondary education. During these times, many young people suffer the loss of friends who just don't "fit" any more. "My friends who went on to college right after high school just don't seem like they have matured," says Julie, 24. "They still live at home. I don't. I've traveled. They haven't. They still go to bars, and I just don't desire that any more. I feel like I am somehow lost, like I don't fit anymore."

This sense of loss increases after postsecondary school graduation. Samantha, 25, had trouble adjusting to the change in her social life after graduation. Throughout college, she focused most of her attention on the groups and activities with which she was involved, but after graduation, she says, "there was no focus in my life. I didn't know what kind of career I wanted and there were no organized activities that I was interested in joining. I felt like I should still be in college, that I was younger than the people at work . . . I found solace in my roommates, creating a surrogate family that I could focus on so I could avoid dealing with my insecurity and fear."[5] An adult spiritual companion can listen to these losses and serve as a connection during this time of disconnection. The companion can ask questions such as: What's it like not having much in common with your old friends? What's it like not feeling comfortable with people at work? Who is a constant in your life? Does your faith in God fit in with any of this?

Another loss that youth often face is the breakup of a dating relationship. This grieving process is a painful one, complicated by confusion, anger, sadness, and loss of confidence. An adult companion or spiritual director can listen, console, and offer hope that there is life after a breakup.

Grief takes on an even more serious tone when a young person experiences the death of someone close in age. Most of the young people I interviewed have lost friends or acquaintances to auto accidents, drug overdoses, extreme sports, suicide, disease, or military service. At times like this, depression can be an issue. In fact, many young people suffer from a depression that has been triggered by loss of a relationship. A young adult needs support from many sources for help through this time. Sometimes peers just don't have the experience or maturity to help, and often young people hesitate to admit to friends that they're depressed. An older adult mentor can provide gentle and wise guidance.

VOCATIONAL ISSUES

Today's young people face a myriad of questions about their vocational paths:

> *There are just too many choices. How do I know what to study?*
> *Am I wasting time in this school?*
> *I want to make the right career choice, but what if I'm wrong? What if I hate the career I choose?*
> *I've seen the generation before me hire people to do life for them. They hire people to care for their children, to clean their house, to landscape their yards. I'm not sure I want to do life*

in that way.
Will I ever be happy in a job, or will it just be work?
My friends have found good jobs. What's wrong with me?
I feel like I'm being called to church work but not called to
being ordained. What are my options? Can I do church work
and still make enough money to pay my bills?
How do I recognize God's call on my life? I'm just not hearing
anything.

One of the privileges of companioning young people is helping them process vocational and job choices. Beth Anderson, vocational associate at Concordia College in Moorehead, Minnesota, observes: "Often college students are programmed since middle school toward a specific career goal. They don't understand that there are other choices. My role is to help them have a broader view, help them think bigger. I often encourage them to go abroad so they can become more globally oriented. This stretches youth like nothing else."

Important goals when directing young people include helping them expand their outlook on life so they will become open to many options. Some youth have a dualistic view about life questions—for them, there's a right answer and a wrong answer and they're just not comfortable with uncertainty. For others, life is predetermined. "God has a plan for me," they declare, "and I need to find what that plan is for my life." This way of thinking can be fraught with fear as young people worry about just what the plan entails—and if they'll ever find it. Whatever their perspective, young people's attitudes toward vocation are often driven by their theology. A spiritual companion needs to tread lightly here, and gently help young people examine their images of God. In fact, much of what a spiritual director—or parent, vocational counselor, or teacher—can do is to offer options, and to give the young person permission to explore alternatives.

Often, youth are afraid of entering the insecurity of today's world. One young woman told me, "I like to spend time with my grandparents and listen to their stories, but later when I get home and watch the news, I get scared. I don't know if the world will be around long enough for me to be a grandparent."

On top of their fear of entering an insecure world, recent graduates of higher education realize that school hasn't prepared them for the real world. They've spent time in a closed, structured environment, with the discipline of classes, papers, and deadlines, and once they have graduated into the world of work, they ask: Now what? Is this all there is? How am I to be in this adult world? What direction should I take with my life, with a job? It's not uncommon for people with four-year degrees to work on construction sites, in fast-food restaurants, or in video stores, often because they're not ready to take on the full responsibility of a professional career.

Balanced between their fear of the future and confusion about the role of an adult is their desire to make a difference in the world. This generation of young people has a high social consciousness. Many have an acquaintance with poverty in their home country or abroad, through church mission trips, study programs, or as visitors. They're far more aware than previous generations of the imbalance of wealth and of political and social repression around the globe. Many young people want their jobs to be meaningful, and they search for a career in which they can help alleviate some of the world's suffering.

As companions help young people with vocational discernment, they also face the challenging task of guiding them as they begin their work lives. In *Ready or Not, Here Life Comes*, pediatrician Mel Levine talks about an epidemic of "work-life unreadiness."[6] Levine relates that several issues emerge when young people begin their first real job. It's not like being in school. There are different expectations, no instant gratification, and little community support. Moreover, a new person on the job must start at the bottom and work up. "Success," Levine writes, "is less dependent on old standbys: athletic ability, coolness, good looks, rote memory."[7]

A spiritual companion can be invaluable as young adults make the transition from postsecondary school to that first real job. A companion or mentor can listen to the frustrations and fears, acknowledge the young person's gifts and talents, boost his or her confidence ravaged by a bad week, and remind him or her of God's constant presence.

Much of the work I do as a spiritual director is in the area of vocation. I've helped young people in a discernment process regarding their course of studies, and I've worked with young directees trying to find meaning in their current occupations. My role is to listen, ask a few key questions, and help my directees believe they can make good decisions. We'll explore the decision-making process further in the next chapter.

PERSONAL IDENTITY

The Reverend Douglas Fenton, staff officer for young adult and higher education ministry in the Episcopal Church, observes that certain identity issues are timeless. Every generation has asked identity questions: Who am I? Where do I fit? As I interviewed young people, other types of personal identity questions emerged:

> *What's it like to be an adult?*
> *Why is everyone else handling this move into adulthood more easily than I am? Am I going to be this helpless for the rest of my life?*
> *My parents keep telling me that I'm going nowhere with my life. I just don't know what I want.*
> *Is the person I am now the person I will be forever?*

There's probably no other time in life more confusing than the time between childhood and adulthood. I can remember when our daughters had "sleepovers." Parents would enthusiastically drop off their teenage daughters at our house. The evening would often begin with what I call "practicing womanhood." The girls would apply makeup, do each other's hair, put on dresses, and generally look ten years older. Often the conversation would revolve around boys and dating and marriage. But as the evening wore on, the girls got younger—more giggly, less adult. And as they rolled out their sleeping bags on our living-room floor, out would come the special stuffed animal or raggedy baby blanket, and the young women were transformed into children again. There's a tension in the adolescent years between acting like adults and needing to retain the safety of childhood. In an article for *Youthworker Journal*, Mary Penner writes, "[I]nstead of defining adolescence as being neither childhood nor adulthood, we must begin to see it as the wonderfully chaotic fusion of both."[8] This period of chaotic fusion we call adolescence is being lengthened in today's Western society. Sociologists observe that adolescence, which has traditionally ended at 18, now extends well into the middle twenties. Author and book critic Lev Grossman writes in *Time Magazine*: "The years from 18 until 25 and even beyond have become a distinct and separate life stage, a strange, transitional never-never land between adolescence and adulthood in which people stall for a few extra years, putting off the iron cage of adult responsibility that constantly threatens to crash down on them."[9] Many of today's "twixters" are taking longer to finish their postsecondary education, putting off marriage, jumping from job to job, and moving back into their parents' home. Older adults—their parents included—wonder what these young people are doing instead of marrying, buying a home, and staying in a career? One answer is that they're searching for who they are and where they fit in society. Jeffrey Arnett, developmental psychologist at the University of Maryland, explains, "This is the one time in their lives when they're not responsible for anyone else. So they have this wonderful freedom to really focus on their own lives and work on becoming the kind of person they want to be."[10] It's a time to be in several relationships, try different jobs, and search for a career that fits their passions and gifts. And it's a time to ask questions:

> *Who am I—really?*
> *What do I want out of life, out of marriage, and out of a career?*
> *The people around me tell me who I am, but I want to know what God thinks. Who does God want me to be?*
> *How do I know that, and how do I grow into that?*

The adolescent and young adult years have classically been the time to question personal identity. This is certainly true of today's youthful seekers.

As young adults ask these questions and struggle with their own identity, they can benefit from interaction with older adults who have made the transition and who can listen, affirm and challenge young adults to search the depths of their being. Moving to a deeper level of being is often a private venture that involves self-reflection and time alone. But youth pastor Steve Wiens points out that today's youth are rarely alone. If they're not actually with people, then they're connected through technology—cell phones, text messaging, e-mail, and instant messaging. Wiens believes that this constant community denies them access to their core. "They have no idea what their core is," he says. "They don't have access to their insides because they're never required to go there." This is where spiritual companionship can help. A companion can invite young people to explore their core—to search deep inside for truth. A series of questions I commonly use with people are:

- What is deep inside you that has been a constant all your life?
- What are your non-negotiable beliefs?
- What are you passionate about?
- Can you sense God in your core? What is that like?
- Who are you called to be?

FAITH ISSUES: IS GOD THE REAL DEAL?
As Jesus approached the villages of Caesarea and Philippi, he asked his disciples this question: "Who do you say I am?" Since that time, two millennia ago, Christians have pondered that same question, and today's youthful seekers are no different. They ask questions such as:

- Who is God in relation to my life, and does it matter?
- Who is Jesus?
- Does religion still matter?
- What is my religion? Do I need one?
- Can I trust God?
- Can I trust the church? There are so many stories of abuse in the news.
- Why do I have to believe in Christ? What about my Muslim friend?
- If I were born in India, I probably would not be a Christian. What does that mean?
- Is Jesus the only way to God?
- Is being a Christian the only way to Jesus?

- The world has told me who I am, but who am I in God? And how do I grow into that?
- What about homosexuality, abortion, euthanasia, and stem cell research?

ARE ALL YOUNG PEOPLE SERIOUS ABOUT FAITH?

Throughout my experience of interviewing youth, youth pastors, parents, teachers, and campus ministers, I received a wide range of answers to the following question: How serious are young people about their faith? Answers run the gamut, ranging from not at all interested, to mildly interested, to actively seeking the life of faith. The following statements illustrate the range of the comments I received regarding youth and their spiritual life:

- Today's youth are too busy with jobs, school, and friends to even consider God.
- Many of today's young adults are turned off by institutional religion and want nothing to do with it.
- Today's youth are cynical about church and religion. Here on the campus at Berkeley, it is more acceptable to come out as a homosexual than to come out as a Christian
- Youth seek religion everywhere they can. They have a plurality of beliefs. They do not believe in one single answer. They are cynical and authentic; hate hypocrisy; are greatly influenced by media.
- Today's youth like to discuss the deeper questions of philosophy, politics, ethics, and religion.
- Today's young adults have a fascination with the old beliefs of prayer and liturgy. There is too much change today. Going back to older ways of doing religion is simpler and more authentic.
- Today's younger generation is very spiritual. They are looking for a mystical experience of God, a heart relationship with God, a changed life, a love of neighbor, and a commitment to a community.

With such diverse responses, those who work with young people are wise to be discerning in their approach. The young are fragile, and are uncertain about what to believe. They can move quickly from a rejection of religion to a longing to have a relationship with God or Jesus. An older adult mentor can provide stability for those who search.

TODAY'S CHRISTIAN CLIMATE

The spiritual issues that young people face are set in the broader context of the contemporary Christian climate. One of the reasons for a wide range of response to the question of youth and faith is the makeup of today's religious culture. Today's postmodern and post-denominational climate is a blend of many paradigm shifts. One is the shift from a Judeo-Christian society to a multi-faith culture. People of other faith traditions have immigrated to Western countries, and global travel has brought people to countries where non-Christian faith traditions are the norm. Today's youth are the most traveled and most globally aware generation in history, and it's no wonder they're asking questions like the one this high school boy posed, "If I were born in India, I would probably be Hindu. So, would I go to heaven?"

Currently, Western society is in a transition from the modern world to a postmodern world. . . . We live . . . in an expanding universe . . . in an interrelationship with all things; and we increasingly communicate through visual and symbolic means. These shifts are resulting in a whole new culture and raise new questions about the way biblical Christianity is to be understood and communicated.
–Robert Webber, *Ancient-Future Faith: Rethinking Evangelicalism for a Postmodern World*, p. 15

At the beginning of the twentieth century, most people in the Western world practiced their faith within the Christian or the Jewish tradition. People were "cradle to grave" members of one denomination, and institutional religion defined their knowledge of God. Reinforced by ethnic traditions and family rituals, their energy was devoted to church activities. One's faith walk was very clear: belong to a specific church and follow its doctrines. While there was security and a sense of belonging, religion was often perceived as something you did on Sunday, with little room for questioning or exploration.

Robert Wuthnow, in *After Heaven: Spirituality in America since the 1950s*, named this "dweller spirituality." One's faith was defined by a specific church—the place where one chose to dwell. Often that place was in one's own neighborhood. That church, or dwelling place, became the social and religious center of a person's life, and rarely did someone defect from the church or the denomination of his or her parents. Wuthnow contrasts dweller spirituality with "seeker spirituality," which began in the 1950s and exists today. As people moved out of ethnic conclaves and into other cities or to suburbs, and as they related to people of other denominations through work, school, social activities, and marriage, they began to question and to search actively for a new church home. Denomination was, for some, low on the list of criteria.

Important factors, instead, were proximity to home, the comfort level of a church, the sense of welcome, the testimonies of friends, quality of children's programs, outreach opportunities, and affinity with the doctrine or theology. By the time the twentieth century ended, a "post-denominational era" was born, and people moved away from the denominational faith of their mothers and fathers. Many Christians, especially youthful Christians, are post-denominational seekers, looking for a faith community that fits their desires, needs, and beliefs.

This seeker mentality sometimes affects the way people talk about faith. The word *religion* is less commonly used than the word *spirituality*. Religion means, to the seeker mind, a set of doctrinal statements of a denomination that people are expected to believe. Religion connotes a governing by the institution of the church. Spirituality, on the other hand, is defined as a person's own awareness of God and, therefore, the person's chosen responses to God. Spirituality is governed by internal motivations and often includes using disciplines such as personal prayer, silence, sacred reading, liturgy, spiritual direction, and social action. Seeker spirituality involves growing in faith as well as practicing faith. A person's choice of a faith community is often based on the people who belong to that community. "I want to grow in my relationship with God and in my knowledge of God, and I want to make the world a better place," says Darren, 28. "Can I do this with the people of this faith community?"

Helping to make the world a better place ranks high on the list for today's Christians. While Christians have always helped the poor and marginalized, the work was most often done by clergy or professional missionaries. Today, large numbers of ordinary people are performing extraordinary service for others. Some go on mission trips at home and abroad. Some use their professional expertise for a set period of time, taking a leave from their jobs to teach, provide medical or dental care, design buildings, or give agricultural or business advice. Some serve in food pantries, work with Habitat for Humanity, or volunteer at senior centers. Many of today's young people eagerly embrace this type of outreach activity.

The experiences bring young people face-to-face with the realities of life, often generating serious questions. A spiritual director, mentor, or an adult companion can journey with youth and be supportive of this process.

It's a challenge to be a seeker in today's Christian climate. This is why faith issues rank high among the issues today's young people face. There are so many choices and they have easy access to an almost infinite amount of information. Books on all aspects of Christianity are prolific. Anyone can go to an online bookstore or a search engine and do a search for words like prayer, faith, or Christianity and find hundreds of choices. That same person can use a search engine and key in the same words. Not only can one find information on the Internet, but a person can "do church" through online church services, chat rooms, blog sites, and daily devotional sites.

Today's media have also gotten into the spirituality act with Christian newspapers and magazines as well as Christian television and radio stations. Christian music is a multimillion-dollar industry. Not to be outdone, the secular press has discovered that religion is news. Network and cable television and the film industry are not shy about portraying Christian themes in their programming.

Today's young people are consumed by the wealth of information. It's no wonder they're searching, no wonder they're sometimes confused, and no wonder they're in need of adult companionship and guidance. Much of the direction I do with young people involves sorting out the messages they are receiving from a multitude of sources. Spiritual director Sandra Gray summarizes this experience when she says, "Youth are overwhelmed by astounding possibilities as they search for truth of the Divine."

MENTORING CHRISTIANS IN TODAY'S CLIMATE

So how does a spiritual director, a mentor, a youth pastor, a teacher, or a parent companion a youth through the faith walk? Listening, being respectful, asking reflective questions, and affirming are the most important components. Today's youth are new at navigating the milieu of Christianity. Some have strong church backgrounds, while others have gone to church only sporadically. And there's a substantial number of young people who weren't raised in a church.

Because of today's wide range of church experience among young people, I often begin a relationship with new directees by inviting them to tell me their faith story. Most tell me about their church backgrounds. Those without a consistent church background will often speak of the churches or youth groups of their friends. Because today's youth communicate so well through story, sometimes this faith story will take many avenues and will last more than one session. Once directees and I are comfortable, I begin to draw them deeper, shifting from religious questions to spiritual questions. How do you sense God's presence in your life? Who do you want God to be for you? How does Jesus fit in with your faith? What's hard for you to believe? What's easy?

I need to confess that when I first began seeing young directees, I was reluctant to ask these probing questions, but once I had enough courage to inquire, the answers flowed freely. It was as if no one in their lives dared to ask these questions, and my directees were intent on answering them. In those early days of companioning youth, the depth of belief as well as the complexity of their lives blew me away. Now I don't hesitate; in fact, sometimes I "push" my young directees harder than my directees who are in midlife. I have found this younger generation to be most comfortable with directness and honesty. They want to be challenged to ponder at a deeper level. But they're also fragile, so I probe and challenge with gentleness, and affirmation, and sometimes laughter.

JOE, 28: Okay, I just don't get it.

Spiritual Director (SD): Don't get what, Joe?

JOE: Why is it that I find my friends so boring?

SD: When did this happen?

JOE: Last week, all my friends wanted to watch the game at the sports bar. I went along with them, but it just wasn't fun.

SD: So what was it like?

JOE: I just didn't drink as much as all of them, and I noticed how obnoxious they all were. They laughed too loud. They told the same jokes I've heard before. I noticed people at the tables around us giving us dirty looks. I was about ready to leave at half-time. I kinda' wished I had. Since then, I've been worried about my reaction. What's wrong with me? Am I turning into a geek?

SD: (laughing) Joe, I don't believe you are turning into a geek, but there's something to this. Okay if we discuss this for a while?

JOE: Sure.

SD: The last few times we met, you have wanted to talk about prayer. You wanted to concentrate on getting closer to God through prayer. How has that been for you?

JOE: (laughing) In a simple phrase, it's worked! I've been able to stay with my prayer practice, and I do feel closer to God.

SD: So what are you noticing about your life?

JOE: Kind of like what we talked about last time. I've noticed that I want to grow in my faith. I really want to become a man of God—whatever that means.

SD: That's great, Joe. So . . . what else are you noticing about your life since the last time we met?

JOE: I really like it when I'm in church. I love the liturgy—the readings, the quiet, the Eucharist. I look forward to going every Sunday, and I notice that I am calmer when I leave.

SD: What's God like during those times?

JOE: God's like—big and expansive. Like when I'm on the lake and I can't see the shore. God's like that—not being able to see the shore. I sometimes feel like I'm going to explode with this expansiveness.

SD: Joe, that's an amazing image of God! What has happened in your prayer time since you have gotten the image of the lake?

JOE: Kind of the same image. I feel the expansiveness of God.

SD: And...

JOE: I feel different, more in tune, like my prayer is getting somewhere or to someone. This is crazy.

SD: Why is it crazy?

JOE: Because I didn't think God was like that. I didn't think He was so real.

Joe: So, tell me again, Joe, what have you been asking for in prayer?

JOE: I want to grow in my faith—Is that what's happening?

SD: Is it?

JOE: (pause) Yes. Guess I have to watch what I pray for.

SD: (laughing) Yes, Joe, it sure sounds like it.

Through several months of spiritual direction, Joe has gradually become comfortable with his process of discovering who God is for him. His spiritual director has stayed with him by listening, pointing out themes, and reviewing his progress. Several months of work came together in this session, and Joe notices that he is becoming who he desires to be. Joe also notices that he is changing. Young people are fearful when they see themselves change, and a spiritual mentor can acknowledge the fear and assure the young person that change is a natural result of spiritual and psychological growth and that God is present in that growth.

God questions are the most-asked faith questions I hear in spiritual direction. Those who have no church background want to know about this God who has the world in such an uproar. Those who have church backgrounds are wondering if the God they learned about in Sunday school and confirmation is the God they want to worship. Many young people equate God with church. If the church hurt me, they reason, God hurt me too. They have the impression that the whole Christian story is represented by their particular church. Some have been taught that to live out Christianity is to follow the rules of a denomination. A spiritual director can help young directees separate church from God and separate Christianity from a particular church. A spiritual director can enable a young directee to see that there's a bigger picture and, most importantly, a director can listen to the God questions: Who is God? Is God real? Does God care for me? Can I trust this God? If there is a God, why is the world in such a mess?

WRAP-UP

As youth look at the religious climate of today—the wealth of information, the hundreds of Christian and non-Christian faith traditions, the religious wars, the opposing opinions—they observe that there are multiple ways to look at God and a myriad of ways to worship and pray to that God. The bottom-line question is: What am I to believe? As a spiritual director, I don't have answers. (I'm still processing that question for myself.) But I can accompany my directees as they search for insight. I can affirm their process. I can gently question and offer suggestions, and I can believe in them.

Notes

1. Michael Rust, "Youth and Faith," infotrac.galegroup.com.floyd.lib.umn.edu.

2. Robert A. Ludwig, *Reconstructing Catholicism for a New Generation* (New York: Crossroad, 1996), 4.

3. Alexandra Robbins and Abby Wilner, *Quarterlife Crisis: The Unique Challenges of Life in Your Twenties* (New York: JP Tarcher/Putnam, 2001), 4.

4. Questions in this chapter are either ones I heard during my interview process or appear in Sharon Daloz Parks, *Big Questions Worthy Dreams: Mentoring Young Adults in Their Search for Meaning, Purpose, and Faith* (San Francisco: Jossey-Bass, 2000), 137–38.

5. Robbins and Wilner, *Quarterlife Crisis*, 99.

6. Mel Levine, *Ready or Not, Here Life Comes* (New York: Simon & Schuster, 2005), 1.

7. Ibid., 7.

8. See www.youthspecialities.com/articles/topics/adolescent.

9. Lev Grossman, "Growing Up? Not so Fast," *Time Magazine*, January 24, 2005, 44.

10. Ibid.

CHAPTER THREE

HANDBOOK OF SPIRITUAL MENTORING: THE SPIRITUAL DIRECTION MODEL

Spiritual mentoring can take many forms: companion, teacher, pastor, leader, coach, supervisor, parent, friend, and spiritual director. You don't need to be a spiritual director to read this chapter. The spiritual direction model is appropriate for many adult-to-youth relationships.

A spiritual director helps people notice God in the complexity, the frustration, and the joy of everyday life. It's a process of asking the questions: What do you sense in your heart. Where is God or Jesus in your life? What's God up to? How do you respond to God? Can you see Jesus in this? A spiritual director helps sort out ideas, emotions, feelings, cultural attitudes, family perspectives, and denominational beliefs. Any aspect of life can be brought into a spiritual direction relationship: questions of faith, relationships, life transitions, major decisions, joys, celebrations, sorrow, anger, grief, confusion, and fear.

> Meeting with a spiritual director is like pushing the pause button on life just long enough to reflect, get honest, and ask, "God where are you in the midst of all this?" so that we might begin to hear God's response and live deeper in the awareness of God's presence.
>
> —Beth Slevcove, Youth Specialties Magalog (Back to School 2004)

A spiritual director is not an advice giver or a counselor, but a gentle presence, a listener and a guide who can help a person notice, discern, and respond to God's invitation to grow, to change, to trust, or to gain freedom. "Spiritual directors allow the Spirit of God to dwell in us and speak through us into a person's life," explains Beth, 26, spiritual director intern. "We embody the beauty, the grace, the mercy, and the love of God into whatever parts of the directee's life that he or she chooses to bring to our time together."

Spiritual direction can take place one-on-one or in a group setting, typically once a month. While listening and asking reflective questions are the main components of spiritual direction, a person can use spiritual direction–type questions in any companion relationship. In other words, one does not need to be a spiritual director to ask spiritual direction questions. Reflective questions can be used in many settings; they encourage a person to probe deeper and to gain clarity.

> The thing my spiritual director does for me which helps me the most is that she affirms me. By this I mean that she lets me know that she sees something good in me right now in the moment. . . .This boosts my confidence in such a way as to help me hear God better and experience God's love for me.
> –Mary, 30

The following dialogue illustrates spiritual direction-type questions:

JULIE, 21, COLLEGE SOPHMORE: I'm just not sure sociology should be my major.

SD: Why do you say that?

JULIE: I don't know. I've just lost interest lately.

SD: In what have you lost interest?

JULIE: I just don't get excited when I think about the subject.

SD: So what happens when you think about sociology?

JULIE: Nothing happens. I'm just not interested any more.

SD: Can you say more about losing interest?

JULIE: Sociology is boring. It's a struggle for me to go to class and to do the reading. I guess it has just lost its appeal to me.

SD: Julie, when you were trying to decide on a major, what appealed to you about sociology?

JULIE: I was fascinated with the relationship individuals have with their culture. I wanted to know more about how society affects a person. Why do some people follow society's way? Why do others go in their own direction?

(pause)

SD: Are you still interested in all those topics?

JULIE: Um ... I guess I am (pause). Yes, I am. But I don't seem to be getting a chance to probe those questions.

SD: Why?

JULIE: The courses I'm taking now are not about those concepts. They're about statistics and ethics.

SD: So ...

JULIE: So I guess I'm not interested in my current courses, but I'm still interested in sociology.

This conversation illustrates a typical spiritual direction session with a college-age person. The following conversation is on the same topic, but it is between Julie and her college advisor, and the approach is different.

JULIE: I'm just not sure sociology should be my major.

ADVISOR: What classes are you currently taking?

JULIE: Statistics, ethics, British literature.

ADVISOR: Is it possible, Julie that you are not interested in your current courses but are still interested in sociology?

JULIE: Yes, that's possible.

The first conversation takes longer than the second, but it invites Julie to come to her own conclusions. The agenda-free questions of the spiritual-direction session allow Julie to revisit the reasons she chose to major in sociology in the first place, and the questions bring back to Julie some of her original enthusiasm, which had been stifled by dry courses.

In the first conversation, Julie's spiritual director didn't have an agenda or any expectations of where the session was going. Questioning without an agenda allowed Julie the freedom to probe her own mind and heart. In the second conversation, the advisor told Julie the answer without allowing Julie to process her thoughts and come to her own conclusion.

You don't need to be a spiritual director to use agenda-free questions. Questions such as: How was that for you? Where did you see God in this situation? Can you say more about this? allow for deeper reflection on the topic.

SPIRITUAL DIRECTION WITH YOUNG DIRECTEES

If you're older than 30, I invite you to pause in the reading of this chapter to reflect on what it was like for you to be in your twenties. Process the following questions in your mind or in your journal.

- What was going on in the world?
- What were your concerns about world events?
- What were your concerns about your relationships, your faith?
- How did you feel about yourself?
- Who were the important people in your life?
- Did you have an adult to companion you? If so what was that like? If not, what would it have been like to have a mentor or a spiritual director?

For some of us, it's been decades since we were in our twenties. Using our imaginations to remember that time of our lives can bring sensitivity and authenticity to our ministry with today's young people. These questions invite us to recall what it was like to be in our twenties so that when we work with people who are young, we don't attempt to project our own midlife concerns on to them. We can be free to appreciate authentically the ideas, energy, enthusiasm, and freshness of someone at the beginning of adulthood.

In my research interviews with young directees, I asked the question: What advice would you give to people who are doing spiritual direction with your age group? Here are their responses:

> *Listen to me, genuinely listen to me (this was the number one response).*
> *Be authentic. Don't be phony.*
> *Take me seriously.*
> *Come with me and notice God with me.*

Stay with me as I try to seek God.
Don't judge.
Don't assume I am like all the other people in my age group.
Don't try to make me into what you are.
Don't give me advice that doesn't reflect knowledge of who I
am.
Help me find where God is in my daily life.
Ask me probing questions.
Affirm me.
Help me see that my anger is directed toward the church, not
God.
Help me process social justice issues.

Those of you who work with midlife directees may notice that many of these points mimic the desires any other age group would have. For spiritual directors who work with young directees, a common piece of advice is: "Treat the younger directee like you would treat any other directee—with the same respect and attention to his or her experience." So is there a difference between doing spiritual direction with a 27-year-old and a 57-year-old? Of course, the answer is yes—thirty years of difference. The younger directee is simply in a different stage of life. The overriding concerns of young people are relationships, career decisions, personal identity, and faith. And though people in midlife or beyond may also be concerned with some of these same issues, the difference is that young people are asking these questions for the first time. This may be one of the first times they have encountered serious difficulties with relationships. This may be the first time they have experienced the death of someone they love. This is their initial experience with higher education and career choices. And, this may be their first crisis of faith. This cluster of "firsts" is what makes spiritual direction with young people unique.

As I write this chapter, in December 2004, the world is concerned with the earthquake in the Indian Ocean and the resulting tsunamis in Sri Lanka, India, Indonesia and Thailand. Three days before the tragedy, my 24-year-old daughter returned from a scuba-diving trip in Thailand—at the exact location of the tsunamis. As she watched the television coverage, she wept over the loss of life. This was her first trip to a poor nation and her first experience with a major disaster involving people she knew. Her questions were: Why did this happen to these gentle people? They were so poor before—what about now? What will happen to them? I don't understand! As her mother, I held her, let her cry, and listened to her grief and confusion. I know this disaster will haunt her for weeks, maybe longer, and I suspect it may even be a pivotal moment in her life.

There's something very powerful about firsts in people's lives. They can become life-changing moments. They can initiate a style or an attitude that remains for years. As youth experience these firsts, they need mature people who can journey with them. They need people who remember the firsts of their own lives and who can listen and encourage and offer hope. An adult companion serving as a spiritual director can assure a young person that with time, life will be better again. An older adult spiritual companion can also provide a historical perspective. During the interview process for this book, I had lunch with a woman in her twenties. The conversation migrated toward what she called "the sad state of the Christian church." I listened for a while and realized that she was born in the early 1980s. She couldn't have had the perspective I had. She couldn't have known the Christian church of the 1950s or the 1960s when Catholics and Protestants were suspicious of one another; when one rarely stepped outside one's denomination; when the world's religious and political leaders would never have dreamed of attending the funeral of a Roman Catholic pope. So I shared a little of my story by talking about the changes I have seen in the Christian church. As I spoke, we both experienced an "aha" moment. She caught a glimpse of the world I came from and saw the forward movement in the church, and with that insight, she gained a sense of hope. And I realized that my role as an older adult is to remind the next generation that the church is responding to God's direction—maybe not as quickly as I'd like, but it *is* responding.

There's much that a middle-aged or older adult can pass on to the youth of today. There is no reason to keep our secrets to ourselves—no reason to hide the gems we've learned about life. But in our companionship with young people, we must be respectful as we offer our sage advice and be open to receiving as much as we give.

Suggestions for Spiritual Directors

In my interviews with spiritual directors who companion young people, I consistently heard advice around the issue of respect and affirmation. My question to those spiritual directors was: What suggestions would you have for adults who companion today's young people? Here are some of the responses I received:

- The most important thing I do is to tell young people that they are loved by God. They are the beloved. Often tears fall, and they begin to talk.

- I provide a safe place for the young person to talk. If the directee expresses anger, I allow that to run its course. I allow tears to flow, and I remain in silent acceptance of the emotion—however it is expressed.

- Be aware of some of the serious issues youth face—issues of relationships, faith, career, and identity.

- Don't assume you know about the issues facing a particular young person. If appropriate, ask the questions. Young directees like to be asked mature questions. "What frustrations do you face in your life?" "What's especially hard for you right now?" "What is important to you." "What about your life is holy?" "What is broken?" "What concerns do you have about today's world?"

- Assure the young directee that it's okay to be living with uncertainty.

- Be patient with directees' questions and paradoxes. Resist the urge to give answers.

- Take young directees seriously. This age group is sensitive to being patronized, and they are very quick to detect phoniness. Be honest. Be real. Be authentic. Youth need mentors and models—authentic people. Authenticity models an authentic God.

- It might be appropriate to do more self-disclosure with younger directees than with your older directees. Youth are looking for a model; they want to know who you are, what you think.

- Remember what it was like when you were 18 or 27. When I first began directing young adults, after having spent years directing people in midlife, I had to adjust to talk about high school and parents who are still authority figures. I also had to be aware of how communal they are and how different that is from my individualistic ways.

- Face your own fears and prejudices about youth. Get past the way they look and talk. Some of my most serious-minded directees had multiple piercings or tattoos. On the other hand, be ready to admit that you may not be able to work with this age group.
- Trust young directees. Trust what they say and what they're learning. Don't be quick to judge.
- Affirm, affirm, affirm. Young people thrive on honest affirmation.

THE VALUE OF STORY

Midway into the ministry of Jesus, he sent out the disciples to teach and to pray. Soon they returned with excitement, "Lord, even the demons obeyed us when we gave them a command in your name!" Jesus listened to their stories. He recognized the value of stories, and he used them in his teaching. Today's young people love stories; they like to hear them, and they are eager to share their faith stories with whoever will listen. In his role as director of young adult ministry for the Episcopal Church, Douglas Fenton meets many young people in his travels. As he engages them in conversation on spiritual matters, they are eager to tell him their stories—they seem to have few opportunities to talk to anyone about their faith.

I had the opportunity to interview four college-age people at a luncheon sponsored by their university. My questions centered on their involvement in their home congregations. About halfway through my interview, one young man interrupted me and asked me to share my story. He wanted to know about the ups and downs of my Christian journey. He wanted to know the "God questions" I ask. Months later, as I conducted more interviews with young people, I found this young man's question a common one. Young people were very interested in my faith journey, and so, when appropriate, I do share stories with my directees. But my stories are short, because I remember that the spiritual direction session is for the directee, not for me.

When working with young directees, I often invite them to tell me stories. I love to say, "Share a story with me about a time when you felt God's presence." When I am working with a directee in the area of vocational discernment, I ask, "Tell me about a time in your childhood when you were really happy about some new adventure." Or "Share with me the story about a real or fictional character you admire." In a time of grieving: "Tell me a story about Jason that made you feel good or made you laugh." Or "Tell me a story about your mom that you will hold in your heart forever." In a time of theological questioning: "Share with me a time when God was very real to you." In a time of identity searching: "Tell me about a time when you felt good about yourself."

Spiritual directors can learn much if they invite directees to share their stories. At the same time, the process of storytelling can give a directee the gift of remembering.

THE SPECIAL ROLE OF SPIRITUAL DIRECTOR TO YOUNG PEOPLE

While spiritual direction is a specific role, I believe other ministries can benefit from the following suggestions:

Listen. As I sit with young directees, I need to remind myself that I am the listener, not the advice giver. My quiet and respectful presence sets a tone that allows them the freedom to share with me.

Slow down and process. Usually I need to help young directees slow down. Generally, they talk too fast, jumping from topic to topic and processing their thoughts in a global and random way. They're high energy, and it's difficult at times not to get caught up in their vigor. Often during a spiritual direction session, I stop the conversation and invite us to be in silence. This slows the pace, allowing each of us to turn to the Holy Spirit for guidance.

Notice themes. Often by the end of a session, a directee has discussed a myriad of topics, so I pull together themes and threads of random thought. This helps the young directee gain clarity.

Encourage new possibilities. Sometimes my role as spiritual director is to encourage my youthful directees to go beyond their scope of possibilities. This requires careful discernment on my part, and I may offer alternate possibilities for them to ponder. For example, I might say, "Daren, what other reasons might be involved in your supervisor treating you in this manner?"

Teach. Sometimes I do some gentle teaching when I'm working with young directees. This is an area where conducting spiritual direction with the young differs from doing direction with people in midlife, and this is particularly true in areas of relationships, prayer, and discernment. Young people simply do not have as much experience with relationships as those who are older. But my teaching style is gentle, I offer alternate options or attitudes, and I am always respectful of the directee's specific experience.

Encourage prayer. In the area of prayer, I notice that my young directees welcome suggestions. Often young people know only one way to pray, and that way has become stale or boring. I make some suggestions and sometimes invite the directee to join me in the practice of that prayer within the context of a spiritual direction session. One directee told me that she really appreciated my prayer suggestions, and she especially liked that I gave her permission to pray in the evening rather than at 6:00 a.m.

Be flexible. Because each person is unique, spiritual directors need to be flexible and open to different approaches. Some young people are reluctant to talk about spiritual matters. They may not have a spiritual language and find it difficult to articulate what they believe. Or they may be examining their beliefs and are afraid to admit that they're seriously questioning Christian doctrines learned in Sunday school or confirmation class. Others are unchurched, wondering what this faith stuff is all about. As a spiritual director, I need to be patient and to ask questions gently. I need to affirm their questions, and I need to remind my young directees of the confidentiality of our relationship.

Seek supervision. Finally, as a spiritual director, it is crucial that I be disciplined in my own prayer and spiritual practices. I need to see my own spiritual director and be supervised by other professional spiritual directors. Supervision has proved invaluable in my work with young directees. When I began to work with my first young person, I sometimes slipped into the role of parent. As I brought this issue to my peer supervision group, they helped me notice that I'd recently become an "empty nester," and was struggling with the loss of my parenting role.

This realization helped me to separate my parenting role from my role as spiritual director. At another meeting of my support group, one of my peers noticed that she felt jealous when working with some of her younger directees because, when she was a youth, she did not have the freedom to ask faith questions. As we helped her process her inner struggles, she gained freedom in this area, and was more open to listening to her directees.

Ultimately, the real spiritual director is the Holy Spirit. I need to remind myself of that truth, and when I enter a direction session, I need to set aside everything I learned about spiritual direction, young adults, postmodernism, and generations, and rely on the guidance of that Spirit. The prayer I say before I enter into all of my spiritual direction sessions is one Gerald May recommends in his book, *Care of Mind, Care of Spirit*: "My prayers are for God's will to be done in you and for your constant deepening in God. During this time that we are together I give myself, my awareness and attention and hopes and heart to God for you. I surrender myself to God for your sake."[1]

TEACHING DISCERNMENT

While all of these guidelines provide excellent advice, one of the most important gifts we can offer to all directees—young and not so young— is the ability to discern. Discernment is about making choices, but it is also about inviting God into that process. Discernment is something people practice all their lives and it grows out of a life of listening to God. Spiritual director and psychologist Lois Lindbloom defines discernment as "The process of paying prayerful attention to one's life in order to be clearer about and more cooperative with God's activity."[2] Spiritual director and group facilitator for the Christos Center spiritual direction preparation program, Lori Gottschalk, further defines discernment as "the art of sensing God's Spirit moving you to respond or react in a particular way. The role of the spiritual director is to listen carefully, and to create an accepting atmosphere in which the person seeking the Spirit's direction can become more aware of and responsive to God's presence."

Guiding a young person through a discernment process involves helping him or her sort out life's many choices. Youth worker and spiritual director Mark Gardner spoke with two former youth group members of his church in White Bear Lake, Minnesota, now college students, who were home during a break. He asked them how the church could have helped prepare them for their move away from home and into the college setting. Both agreed that they wished they'd learned how to sort through the voices they heard (parents, teachers, friends, the church, advertising media, and college recruiters) as they were in the decision-making process. They wanted to know how they could hear God's voice in the midst of the other voices, and they wished they had learned some discernment tools.

There are many techniques or tools in the discernment process. Within the context of a concrete situation, let's look at discernment techniques that are particularly helpful when working with teens and twentysomethings.

Jason is 18 and is asking his spiritual director about a decision to get into a serious relationship with his girl friend.

JASON: I want to ask Lori to be in a serious relationship with me.

SD: Go on.

JASON: Well, it's been two months since Kristin broke up with me. I'm over that and am ready to be in relationship again.

SD: And ...

JASON: I like Lori.

SD: What do you like about Lori?

JASON: She's funny. We laugh a lot when we're together. We have fun when we're with friends and when we're alone. We have good conversations.

SD: Say more, Jason, about the laughter and the good conversations.

JASON: Well, we laugh at the same things—like the stuff we see on TV, and we like the same movies. And we like to talk about lots of stuff.

SD: What kinds of stuff do you like to talk about?

JASON: Oh, you know, the usual stuff: our friends, plans for after high school, our jobs. Sometimes we talk about deeper stuff.

SD: What deeper stuff?

JASON: We talk about what we want to do with our lives. We talk about the way the world is today. We talk about God—what we think God is like.

SD: So how does it feel, Jason, when you are talking about the deeper stuff when you are with Lori?

JASON: It feels good. Like I haven't been able to talk about this stuff with anyone else—even my best friend, Rob.

SD: Why is that?

JASON: I'm not sure. It just feels right to talk to her about that stuff. She seems to understand me.

SD: So, you like Lori, you can laugh and have fun when you are together, and you can talk about deeper issues. So, Jason, why the reluctance to ask her to be in a serious relationship?

JASON: I don't know (pause). It just doesn't feel right (pause). I'm wondering if it's too soon after Kristin?

SD: Let's try something, Jason. Imagine asking Lori to be in a serious relationship with you, and she says yes. Can you do that?

JASON: Yes.

SD: So how do you feel?

JASON: Great. Happy that she thinks I'm important in her life.

SD: Okay, so imagine what your life would be like if you were in a serious relationship with Lori.

JASON: Well, we could be together a lot. I wouldn't have to worry about dating other girls. I would always be with her. I would fit in more with my friends.

SD: Jason, say more about fitting in.

JASON: Well, Zack and Ian have serious girlfriends. So we could always do stuff together.

SD: Okay, Jason, now imagine your life if you did not ask Lori to be in a serious relationship with you?

JASON: (pause) Well, I guess I would be free to date around, but I'm not too good, you know, with asking girls out. I guess I could still do stuff with Zack and Ian. I wouldn't need to spend all my time with Lori.

SD: Jason what are you feeling?

> JASON: I don't know (pause). Maybe, freer somehow. I just don't know.
>
> SD: Can you try to describe "freer"?
>
> JASON: (pause) I guess it's like I could have both. I could date Lori when I wanted to, but if I didn't want to, I wouldn't have to. It just feels better somehow.
>
> SD: Jason, is God anywhere in this?
>
> JASON: Yeah, God is here. I think God wants me to wait for a while.

Notice that the spiritual director leads Jason in a discernment process. The director invites Jason to use his imagination to go to a deeper level—to a feeling level. It helps Jason be in touch with a deeper place or, as we spiritual directors like to say, "his inner movements." This discernment process brings Jason to an authentic and honest decision.

Another technique the spiritual director could have used would have been to ask Jason if he says "yes" to being in a serious relationship with Lori, what would he say "no" to? Following is an example of the "yes-no" discernment technique. This situation is centered on helping a directee affirm a decision she has already made.

> TAMMY (24): Two of my best friends graduated from college last week, and I'm feeling kind of bad about that.
>
> SD: Describe "feeling bad."
>
> TAMMY: Well, I'm still over two years away from graduation. I could have been done and started on my career. Now I'm still working at this dumb clinic job and slowly getting my degree.
>
> SD: Tammy, you said "no" to finishing your degree in four years. But what have you said "yes" to? What have you done instead?
>
> TAMMY: Well, of course, I spent three months back packing around Europe. I wouldn't trade that.
>
> SD: Tammy, we've talked about your European adventure before. Can you just summarize what you gained from that period in your life?

TAMMY: Wow . . . where do I start? I learned a lot about myself. I did things I thought I could never do. Really gave me more self-confidence. I met so many people from other countries and learned so many different attitudes on life. I still e-mail some of the people I met.

SD: That's great, Tammy. What else have you done that you couldn't have done because you didn't go directly on to school?

TAMMY: I was able to move out and live on my own right out of high school because I had this good-paying, full-time job.

SD: What opportunities has living on your own presented?

TAMMY: It hasn't been easy, but I look at myself and see that I'm much more mature than Rachael and Sara. They still live at home. I know how to budget my money. They still want to go to bars and hang out. I lost interest in that last year. It's a waste of time and money.

SD: So, let's switch gears. Tammy, what if you had said "yes" to finishing your degree in four years?

TAMMY: I guess I would have just graduated last month.

SD: What would that have been like?

Tammy: It would have felt good, I guess . . . but I don't know (pause).

SD: You don't know about what?

TAMMY: (pause) Well, I still really don't know what I want to do in life. I still don't really have a major. If I had gone right to school, I probably would have just chosen a major just to choose a major.

SD: And, how does that feel?

TAMMY: Oddly enough, it feels irresponsible. Wow, I didn't expect that! I would have wasted my parent's money and have had all those loans to pay back—but for what?

SD: Tammy, can you summarize what we have just discussed?

TAMMY: Okay. I said "no" to doing my degree in four years, and this has given me an opportunity to travel and to meet people and to grow up. If I had said "yes," I wouldn't have had those opportunities, and I would have wasted lots of money.

> SD: So how does that make you feel?
>
> TAMMY: I guess I'm smarter than I thought I was (laugh).
>
> SD: One more question, Tammy: Do you see God in any of this?
>
> TAMMY: I sure do. I really prayed about this decision to do my degree slowly and to travel, and I think God did guide me, because now I think I made a good decision.

In this example, the spiritual director guided Tammy in examining her discernment process—certainly a valid way to teach discernment. The spiritual director let Tammy do the work. She invited Tammy to delve deeper into her feelings by asking the first question, "Describe feeling bad." She asked Tammy to summarize the session rather than doing it for her. Finally, through asking simple, open questions, the spiritual director invited Tammy to search her heart for her motivations.

OTHER DISCERNMENT TOOLS

There are special questions I ask directees that help in the discernment process. If my directee has some experience in decision making, I ask,

- How have you discerned in the past?
- How has God guided you in your decisions before?
- Tell me about other decisions you have made in your life.
- How have you made them?
- Does this particular decision give you a sense of wholeness, integration, or energy?
- How detached are you concerning the outcome?

Some other helpful questions include:

- Does this decision make you feel better or worse?
- Does this decision cause you to love God, yourself, and others more?
- What happens when you pray about this?
- Do you sense God's presence or love?
- Imagine if your best friend were in this situation. What

questions would you ask him or her? What advice might you give to him or her?

As I help directees with the discernment process, I want to know if others are helping them with their decision, so I ask, Who else's advice are you seeking? Do you have others who can help you with your decision? What kind of messages are you getting from others? What doors are opening for you? A college student e-mailed a group of people who had served as mentors to her over the years and asked them to serve as her advisory board. When she was in a career discernment process during her senior year, she consulted that board for advice. They encouraged her to watch for invitations in her life. When she acted on their advice, she began to notice opportunities and could sift through them with ease. After going through this period of discernment, she concluded, "Sometimes all it takes is for a friend, parent, professor, employer, or mentor to recognize an ability or gift that we have. This can really spark our interest and enable us to move on a passion that we have failed to recognize."

Vocational Discernment

The previous section focuses on one of the key issues young people face: career and vocational choices. In working with people who are in their twenties, I notice much angst surrounding school and career choice. There are too many choices and too much information coming from too many directions. As I listen to these young adults, I ask questions that can help them be aware of their core interests and talents. I encourage them to talk to people who know them and can help them discern. And I invite them to seek God's guidance.

In many of my interviews with young people, I've noticed that most want their vocational decisions to affect some change in the world. Some of these young people refer to a vocation as a call from God. The word *call* is a good one because it invites God into the process. I often use that word when I'm working with people seeking their first career. Spiritual director and pastor Emily Hegner Rova of Bremerton, Washington, created a series of questions for students at a Lutheran seminary to help with their discernment process. Here are some of them:

- How has God been a part of the life decisions you've had to make?
- Do you have a sense of call from God?
- Is there some thread of interest that has run throughout your life?
- As you pray about your career questions, what do you sense God saying?
- What gives you energy, freedom, and life? Or what drains life from you?
- What are the places in your life where you get "lost" doing what you are doing? You lose track of time?
- What have others said to you about your gifts and abilities?[3]

A word of caution here: Spiritual directors are not vocational counselors. Educational institutions and private practices have a number of well-prepared career and vocational counselors who employ a variety of tools to help identify career goals. Don't hesitate to refer directees to these people. The role of spiritual companion is to bring the directee to a deeper level of discernment and to invite the Spirit into the process.

DISCERNING FAITH ISSUES

Discernment isn't always about life decisions. It can also be about moral, ethical, or theological beliefs. Often these issues emerge in a spiritual direction relationship. The director is to listen, ask agenda-free questions, and point the directee toward God. Sometimes, a spiritual director helps the young directee sort out his or her beliefs. Young people, without years of experience sorting out attitudes, are often susceptible to the attitudes of society, friends, media, parents, teachers, church youth leaders, employment supervisors, and coaches. Much of the growing-up process is claiming one's own beliefs, so the methods a young person learns from a sensitive older adult can set a tone for future decision making.

So how can an adult companion enable a youth to be discerning in ethical, moral, or theological beliefs? An older adult must first listen. Allow the young person to express his or her attitudes and beliefs. Ask clarifying questions, questions that help the directee focus on the issue. If it seems appropriate, draw the youth into a reflection on the ramifications of those beliefs. When I work in this area of beliefs, I need to be very discerning during the direction session. I need to be respectful of a person's beliefs, yet if those beliefs have the potential of danger, I need to help the person realize that potential danger.

PRAYER AND THE NEW GENERATIONS OF CHRISTIANS

Ultimately, my goal in working with all my directees, young and not so young, is to enable them to have an ongoing, clear, honest connection with God. Remaining in the heart of God is an awesome discernment tool. Therefore, I lead people in two areas: noticing God in prayer and noticing God in the everyday activities of life. I often begin the discussion by asking questions such as:

- How do you pray?
- Where do you pray?"
- What's it like to be in prayer?
- Do you pray to God or Jesus?
- Would you rather pray alone or with others?
- What or who helps you with prayer?
- When do you feel closest to God, or Jesus, or the Spirit?
- Are you satisfied with your prayer?
- Where did you learn to pray?
- How is God, or Jesus, or the Holy Spirit present in your life?
- Do you sense God in ordinary events of life?

Based on the conversation generated by these questions, I can move on in the session. Sometimes directees are not praying, or rarely praying, or are bored with prayer. In that case, I help them explore their history of prayer: where they learned to pray, their attitudes toward prayer, and their successes/failures with prayer. Often directees believe in only one way to pray based on what they learned from parents or from church. My role is to gently open up new vistas of prayer for the directee or to affirm that what the directee is doing is prayer. In the previous example of Joe (see chapter two, pages 34–35), the young man who experienced God as an enormous lake, I had several sessions with him about prayer. During the course of those sessions, the key question I asked him was, Where do you experience God? What's that like? It's no surprise that Joe experienced God through nature, but he never realized that, as he marveled at the beauty of nature, he was praying.

Sometimes directees have little or no experience with church and prayer. Yet they're coming to me for guidance on how to satisfy a hunger for "something more." In those cases, I find out how much they do know, and I go from there.

Many of today's youth desire an experiential relationship with God or Jesus, and they're comfortable noticing God in all areas of their lives. "I feel God's presence when I'm studying or when I'm at the coffee shop with my friends or even at my job, which I hate," says Ben, 27. "God gets me through the day." As we learned in chapter one, youth are comfortable with mystery, and I've noticed that they don't need to analyze or prove their experience with God or with Jesus. They just know. They're okay with the mystery of the Holy Presence. They are, however, reluctant to discuss sacred experiences with just anybody. An adult companion can listen and affirm as young people begin to talk about their experiences with God.

This hunger for the experience of God allows young people to be comfortable with images they can see and feel. "I have a poster of a snowboarder in the Rockies in my bedroom," says Grant, 23, from Colorado. "Every time I look at it, I'm reminded of what it felt like to be snowboarding in the mountains—how I felt God's presence there. That poster brings me back to that time. It's awesome!" Part of my work as a spiritual director is to encourage young people to seek out their own sacred images and sacred places. I may even offer some suggestions. I have found young people to be comfortable with objects such as candles, crosses, pictures, shells, rocks, branches, flowers, clay pots, pinecones, woodcarvings, and children's books. Sometimes I encourage individual directees or groups (if I'm doing group spiritual direction) to choose something that will draw them into prayer. I invite them to use that object to help with prayer, and we process that experience the next time we meet.

I frequently encourage young people to use the Gospels as a way to connect with Jesus in prayer. I invite them to imagine themselves in a gospel story and to observe Jesus. What is Jesus doing? How is he with the people around him? What do you sense about Jesus? How do you feel by being in his presence? Can you talk to Jesus? Can you listen as he talks to you? Gospel stories that especially appeal to young people are:

> Jesus Heals a Paralyzed Man: Luke 5:17–26
> Jesus and Zacchaeus: Luke 19:1–10
> Jesus Heals the Roman Officer's Servant: Luke 7:1–10
> Jesus Feeds 5,000: Matthew 14:13–21
> Jesus Blesses the Children: Mark 10:13–16
> The Boy Jesus in the Temple: Luke 2:41–51
> Jesus Heals a Crippled Woman on the Sabbath: Luke 13:10–17

I'm not opposed to doing some gentle teaching when I work with younger directees. Often, that teaching is accompanied by practice. After several sessions with Megan, she asked me to help her with her prayer, which for her had become rote and boring. Knowing that Megan was somewhat comfortable with scripture, I taught her *lectio divina*, or sacred reading. Often, people know how to study scripture, but don't know that scripture can be used as prayer. I explained the method to her and asked if she wanted to sample it. She agreed, so I chose a short passage of scripture and invited her to close her eyes and listen as I read it a few times—pausing for silence after each reading. I invited her to notice what word particularly spoke to her or to notice what she was feeling. Knowing that Megan's life was particularly busy, I chose the line from Psalm 23, "He leads me beside still waters. He refreshes my soul." In our conversation afterwards, Megan said the scripture passage brought her peace. She saw the still water and could imagine sitting by it. I encouraged her to mentally go back to that place when her life became frantic.

Prayer for youth needs to be simple and experiential. That's why the classic prayer disciplines of *lectio divina*, the Ignatian method, the Jesus prayer, and breath prayer appeal to today's younger generations.

I know of one church in Illinois that set up prayer stations for their high school youth group. They partitioned off the large meeting room into several small "cubby holes," each with a theme. One contained pictures of natural beauty. In another there were boxes of sand with objects such as shells, stones, and twigs. In a third was a finger labyrinth. In another spot, there were some scripture verses and words from Christian writers. Another place had clay. Another station had cardboard and collage material. Another had a few children's books such as *The Velveteen Rabbit* and *Frederick*, and some beanbags for sitting. The youth were invited to silently visit some of the areas and to touch and play with the objects. They were to open themselves to prayer or to think about how God is present to them through the object. It was a successful evening; at the end of it, the participants shared their experiences with the enthusiasm that indicated they were happy to immerse themselves in the stuff of prayer. As soon as stories of this prayer experience trickled down to the rest of the congregation, the youth leaders were asked to allow the prayer stations to remain for several days so adults had the opportunity to experiment with prayer in this manner.

PRAYER 24-7

While many young people today are drawn to the more contemplative forms of prayer, often that quiet prayer leads to intercession. Intercessory prayer is prayer on behalf of someone or on behalf of a situation. One of the most amazing stories I encountered as I conducted my research was the 24-7 prayer movement. It began in Chichester, England, in September 1999, and rapidly spread around Europe, then internationally. Young people gather in small prayer rooms in various settings and pray nonstop, around the clock. They intercede for cities, nations, world leaders, the church, AIDS, those addicted to drugs, and for personal situations. Pete Greig, who laid the groundwork for the first prayer space, describes the first time he tried this idea in his church in Chichester. He knew he wanted a sacred space for the people who were praying, so he asked some of the artists in his congregation to make a small room, adjoining the church offices, into a space conducive to prayer.

> *The first time I stepped into the room, I was amazed. . . . By draping linen and placing lamps, they had divided the room into distinct areas with scatter cushions on the floor and paper covering the walls awaiting our clumsy graffiti. In one area they had laid out coffee facilities, and on the wall was a large local map. There was an altar built around the old pool table*

covered in tea lights, a Bedouin style tent made from white muslin sweeping down from the ceiling, and in one corner, the branch of a tree studded with twinkling white lights. I noticed that the windows had been blacked out for privacy, and someone had already pinned a hand-written prayer to the branch of the tree. Even before the hours of prayer that would fill this room and before the walls were covered in artwork expressing people's heart cries to God, this was now a room that made you want to whisper.[4]

Once the sacred space was created, young people signed up for shifts to come and pray. Some learned to use *lectio divina*, some used liturgical prayer books, others wrote prayers on paper, and some created art as prayer. Word of mouth resulted in young people coming to Chichester to pray, then returning to their homes and creating similar prayer spaces. A Web page was created, and the 24-7 prayer idea was released to the world. At the same month and year that the 24-7 prayer movement was starting in Chichester, England, a similar movement began in Kansas City, Missouri—the International House of Prayer (IHOP). Neither knew of the other.

The 24-7 prayer movement began with young people—people with the energy and passion to look at today's world and to want to pray actively for its problems. Roger Ellis, a long time member of the 24-7 prayer movement, reflects, "The heart of 24-7 is to bring power and mission together and to do this in a way, which flows out of the instincts and culture of the emerging generations. . . . Run by a bunch of nobodies, surfing the 'waves of the Spirit' and making it up as they went along. The rest is history."[5]

BEING A COMPANION TO THOSE WHO PRAY

When people, young and old, actively engage in prayer, something within them changes. Pete Greig noticed this in the midst of the 24-7 movement. "Prayer is not just about the contemplative moments or the moments when I'm consciously firing words at God," he says. "The call to 'pray without ceasing' (1 Thessalonians 5:17) is a call to remember Christ's presence continually in the subconscious as well as the conscious realms. . . . The ultimate 24-7 prayer room is the human heart fully surrendered to God and not a room full of coffee mugs and hand-drawn pictures!"[6]

When a person makes a serious commitment to prayer, the heart surrenders to God, and the person looks at life differently. The person becomes more like Jesus in action and in attitude. Like Joe, the young man in chapter two, who noticed that he no longer enjoyed sitting in a bar with his friends, people's attitudes and desires and likes and dislikes change. In times like that, a young person needs an older adult who's been through these transitions. A spiritual mentor can listen to the confusion surrounding these changes and can help the young person look at what is happening. A spiritual companion can assure the young directee that this is a normal progression towards Christian maturity. Surrendering to God and allowing one's heart to be changed is spiritual formation, but it cannot happen in a vacuum. A person needs companions along the way.

Praying for Those You Companion

Included in the privilege of mentoring young people is the sacred call to pray for them. A spiritual director/companion who is aware of the needs of a young person can bring those needs before God in prayer. Sometimes, however, a companion does not know the concerns of the young in his or her life, or he or she may not be aware of all ramifications of the issues surrounding a young person's life. One prayer form I like to use in these situations is a form of the classic Jesus prayer, "Lord Jesus Christ, son of the living God, have mercy on Jason." Or, "Jesus, bring forgiveness to this situation." Or, "God, bring peace and healing to this family." These phrases can be repeated often throughout the day in such a way that the inner soul is constantly in prayer.

Whether or not I am aware of all the issues facing my young directees, I always pray a prayer of protection for them. Youth have a tendency to place themselves in harm's way through experimentation with drugs and alcohol, extreme sports, reckless driving, and just generally diving into something before thinking. In addition, corruption, dishonesty, and evil surround them. Whether this evil is a spiritual force or the result of the cruel intentions of others, there are unhealthy events and attitudes that can trap people, especially the young. I use Psalm 91 all the time. I pray that psalm for my own children, for my ministry, for my colleagues, and for the young people in my life.

While much of my prayer is done in private, I join my congregation in prayer for our young during the weekly liturgy. Special times of the year lend themselves to this practice: prayer for children as they begin school or before summer vacation, or for pilgrims or those going on a mission trip. I pray for my directees in their presence. I end each spiritual direction session with prayer, and I have noticed that all my directees, young and not so young, like that personal prayer.

I have also noticed that the more I practice prayer, the more I realize that it is not the technique or the words that are important. It is the intent—the honest and loving desire to hold someone before God and to ask for guidance, peace, protection, and healing.

COMPANIONING YOUTH IN A GROUP SETTING

So far, we've focused on individual or one-on-one spiritual companionship. But because of the communal nature of today's teens and twentysomethings, group spiritual direction is a workable—and sometimes a preferred—option. In some cases, today's young people feel more comfortable and not as vulnerable in a group setting. They can better process their ideas and questions within the context of a group. Sister Patricia McCulloch, youth minister in a large Catholic Church, observes,

> *I have ministered with teenagers for some eighteen years. I have worked among the rich and the poor; in suburbs, cities, and small towns; in the United States and Venezuela. I have come to know that young people possess a very strong and deep spirituality. Their difficulty lies in finding the language to express it. . . . [G]roup spiritual direction offers young people an opportunity to put words on what is happening in their lives.*[7]

In my interviews with people who work with youth, I asked this question of a number of adults who facilitate group spiritual direction with high school students: What motivates youth to come to group direction? Spiritual director Brenna Jones of Wheaton, Illinois, said that her group simply liked being listened to, not just by their peers but also by an adult. They liked talking about and being guided into deeper "life stuff." Spiritual director Mark Gardner of White Bear Lake, Minnesota, agreed: "Youth like to be listened to and have their questions and opinions respected. They want opportunities to talk, about issues of faith and life, with peers and adults."

So what issues do youth like to discuss in a group setting? "Absolutely everything," says Gardner. "The joys and frustrations of faith, questions about other religious beliefs (and who is right), questions about their purpose in life, questions about how to make faithful decisions, questions about anger and confusion with God." Jones adds that relationships are most often discussed. Guy-girl relationships are number one with peer, parental, and sibling relationships included in the mix.

FORMATS FOR GROUP SPIRITUAL DIRECTION

Silence. Most of the spiritual directors I interviewed like to begin with a time of silence to enable the youth to focus on how God has and has not been present in their lives. Most facilitators admitted that it is a challenge to get the group to be quiet. It helps to meet in a small, informal, quiet room with dimmed lights and a candle. Some begin with a little music such as Taizé music or a short passage of scripture or other sacred reading. Some facilitators invite the group to reflect on the days since the group last met. Most groups then move into a brief period of check-in. How have you been since we last met? What was a high point for the week, a low point? What are you looking forward to in the coming week? Where did you experience God this week? How are you feeling right now? After the check-in, each person has an opportunity to talk about his faith journey. What has been hard for you? What is new? What's God up to in your life? Where has God been missing? Where in your life do you hope for Jesus' presence?

Listening and sharing. The method that works best for those
I interviewed is to have everyone listen to the presenter—no
interruptions. The group direction facilitators I interviewed said
this was even more difficult to achieve than quieting the group
at the beginning. So, the facilitators had to be creative. One
facilitator uses an object, a funky-looking stuffed bird that she
passes to the designated speaker. The person holding "funky
bird" is the only one who can talk. The others listen. After the
designated speaker finishes, the group is invited to focus on that
person's sharing; using agenda-free questions. How did you feel
when your brother said that to you? Did you pray about this?
What's God saying to you now? The questions are directed to
the speaker. Advice or personal stories (such as, When this
happened to me, I . . .) are not allowed.

After a period of time, the next person speaks. Encouraging
agenda-free questions took some time and some modeling by
the facilitator. But with practice, most of my interviewees said
their groups "got it." All of the facilitators I interviewed end
their group spiritual direction session with more silence, and
then they pray for each other.

Attentiveness to the Holy Spirit. My interviewees admitted
that the above format was subject to minute-by-minute change.
It is essential for the facilitator to remain attentive to the Spirit
throughout the session. Some sessions work well; others become
somewhat chaotic. But in answer to my final question—Is it
worth it?—I could see the facilitators believe that God is very
much present in each session—no matter what happens. Brenna
Jones observed, "At times there was such an abundance of
unconditional love and acceptance in the room, that warmth
and peace were almost palpable."

All the spiritual directors I interviewed were new to group direction with young people. Some even named their participation "experimental." So I asked them for observations and advice for others who are bold enough to also experiment.

Observations

- I don't think I was prepared for the way in which my group of young people experienced their spiritual lives together in community. I have become more starkly aware of how individualistic I am about my relationship with God. I just don't think about it in community the way these people do.
- After a two-hour meeting with my group of young people, with all their energy and questions, I was exhausted.
- I was surprised by the openness, honesty, and courage youth demonstrated in talking about deeply personal issues of faith and life.
- I was amazed by the number of youth who participated—and came back week after week.
- The parents surprised me. They were excited. One parent commented, "I don't know exactly what you talked about, my son said it was confidential, but I can tell it's making a difference in his life."

Suggestions

- Honor the deep spirituality of youth today.
- Dive bravely and without apology into different prayer forms.
- Put your own God box aside, and be ready to have your faith challenged to its very core.
- Pray constantly for the youth in the group and for yourself—especially as you lead the group.
- Have your own spiritual director.
- Recognize that the group may go off into many tangents and that some sessions may become conversational, or advice giving, or storytelling.
- Consider the popular culture (music, movies, television, advertisements, sports) as appropriate topics. The spirituality

of young people is grounded in these "secular" experiences (where God is diligently at work).

- If you are doing group direction within a church setting, communicate clearly with the youth director, youth committee, and pastors. If you are in a college or seminary setting, communicate with the campus minister or chaplain. Encourage those leaders to be a part of a group spiritual direction experience.

- Pay attention to your "faith language." You might need to translate the language of prayer and spirituality into language that works for young people.

- Consider using some sort of screening process. Some young people are just not ready for group spiritual direction.

- Encourage more adults in the church to be involved in spiritual direction so there is more understanding about what you are attempting with the youth.

SPONTANEOUS SPIRITUAL DIRECTION

As I spoke with people who work with high school youth, they admitted that spiritual direction—either group or individual—often happens spontaneously. It's rare for a high school student to actually schedule an appointment to see a spiritual director. Megan, a youth pastor in Chicago, Illinois, remarked that she does a lot of spiritual direction in the hallway after the youth meeting or on the bus going to a youth event. She taught herself to be ready to go into a spiritual direction mode at any time. Spiritual director and college vocational counselor Beth Anderson says, "Young people move from one thing to another quickly. The spiritual direction relationship with young adults is not often regular and ongoing, but sporadic. Students tend to seek out spiritual direction on an as-needed basis rather than on a regular schedule."

Nor do spiritual companion relationships always happen in a church or school setting. Several people told me they act as spiritual companions when they chaperone mission trips, accompany high school students on the band bus, or sit in a coffee shop. These relationships are often not long term, but they can be. One seminary student admitted to me that she couldn't kick the cigarette habit, and she didn't want anyone in seminary to know she smoked, so she studied off campus. She intentionally drove to a restaurant several miles from the seminary every evening to study. Without knowing, she chose a restaurant that was a hangout for high school students who smoked. "About twice a week I was joined by kids who just wanted to talk," she says. "Often they were the same kids every time. When they found out I was in seminary, the God questions poured out of them. It felt like group spiritual direction. I guess they felt safe with me."

WRAP-UP

"I guess they felt safe with me." The spiritual mentoring of today's young people involves trust. Young people want to know if they can risk sharing their honest thoughts and feelings with us. It is not hard to win the trust of today's hungry souls if we can be honest, authentic, and interested. I've talked to one of the high school girls who "hung around" my seminary friend who studied off campus, so I know the impact she had on those kids. Granted, my friend wasn't being authentic by hiding her smoking habit from other seminary students, but she was honest with the kids in the restaurant. She listened to their stories, asked them questions, looked them in the eye, and sometimes lovingly teased them. I've lost contact with my friend, but I hope she's doing youth ministry somewhere. She's got what it takes.

NOTES

1. Gerald May, *Care of Mind, Care of Spirit* (New York: HarperCollins, 1992), 121.

2. Lois Lindbloom, *Is That You God?: Cultivating Discernment as a Way of Life* (Northfield, MN: Lois Lindbloom, 2004), 1.

3. See www.fishernet.net111?godlead.

4. Pete Greig and Dave Roberts, *Red Moon Rising: How 24-7 Prayer Is Awakening a Generation* (Orlando, FL: Relevant Books, 2005), 60.

5. Ibid., ii.

6. Ibid., 192–93.

7. Patricia McColloch, "Group Spiritual Direction with Teenagers," *The Lived Experience of Group Spiritual Direction*, ed. Rose Mary Dougherty (Mahwah, NJ: Paulist Press, 2003), 198.

CHAPTER FOUR

SPIRITUAL MENTORING IN A CHURCH SETTING

It's Thursday of Holy Week. The community has gathered at half past seven for the solemn evening service. The lights are dimmed, candles glow. After the reading of the Gospel—the moving words of Jesus' washing the disciples' feet—students in the Journey to Adulthood class (grades 6–12) go to the front of the church, pour water into bowls, gather towels, and wait, on their knees, for members of the congregation to come and have their feet or hands washed. It's a moving scene—young people on their knees, eager to be servants, like Jesus washing the feet of his disciples. After the service, the same group of young people stay up all night, taking turns praying in the candlelit chapel, keeping watch on behalf of the congregation. For members of that J2A class, this is a pivotal moment of the church year as they willingly undertake a vital role on one of the most holy days of the liturgical calendar.

PARTICIPATING IN THE LIFE OF A CHURCH

In chapter one, I pointed out that many of today's youth are serious about their faith walk, and many opt to stay within churches to practice their faith. But within the context of the church, they have a passionate desire to participate in the life of the community. In addition to that communal life, many young people desire faith experiences, are comfortable with images and symbols, and welcome mystery. In the Maundy Thursday service, the youth of St. John's Episcopal Church in Minneapolis, Minnesota, were able do it all.

I had an opportunity to sit with these young people after the Holy Thursday service and before the prayer vigil began, and I asked them what was meaningful about tonight's service and why were they doing it. Practically all twenty-eight of them enthusiastically responded:

PATRICK, 14: *I like putting myself with Jesus. It makes it easier to go on with my life knowing what he went through.*

CARTER, 12: *This service was powerful; the total silence is humbling; feels like you are reliving a part of history.*

AMOS, 17: *This service reminds me that God is with us whenever we need him. Tonight is about showing this companionship with him. It is when he needs us the most.*

MEGGIE, 18 (whose family came home early from a week of vacation so she and her brother could participate in the service): *It is an intentional time to go through the motions, to physically experience the story of Jesus' last days. Being here tonight is so different than regular life.*

KIT, 13: *It is a time to reflect on yourself and to feel in tune with community.*

MATTHEW, 14: *It's fun to be in the church all night, but it is also peaceful and calm.*

BONNIE, 13: *Tonight helps me understand the meaning of Easter. It allows me a chance to give back of myself.*

HOW CHURCHES ATTRACT AND KEEP YOUNG PEOPLE

It's obvious that the church in this Holy Thursday story is doing something to keep its young people involved. It respects and values its youth enough to invite them to take an important role on one of the most holy of days. Keeping young people interested and active in church is a challenge in today's culture. In *Reconstructing Catholicism for a New Generation*, Robert Ludwig writes: "The irony is that today's young people exhibit simultaneously a distrustful distancing from institutional religion and a new openness to spirituality and profound human values."[1]

He expresses a hope that churches become aware of the spiritual hunger of youth, citing a Gallup report on the six basic needs of young people:

- The need to believe that life is meaningful and has a purpose
- The need for a sense of community and deeper relationships
- The need to be appreciated and loved
- The need to be listened to—to be heard
- The need to feel that one is growing in faith
- The need for practical help in developing a mature faith[2]

In her article, "What Attracts and Keeps Students at Your Church," Kara Powell reports on a study conducted by Carol Lytch in her book *Choosing Church: What Makes a Difference for Teens.* Lytch studied young people in three churches in Louisville, Kentucky—one mainline Protestant, one Roman Catholic, and the third Evangelical. She attended church services, youth meetings, retreats, Bible studies, and small group meetings. She visited with and interviewed many young people, and the results of those interviews indicated three factors that attract and keep young people in church:

1. *A sense of belonging.* Young people who felt at home and safe in their churches and with their youth activities were most likely to stay actively involved in church.
2. *A sense of meaning.* Young people were more likely to keep coming back if youth activities were filled with meaningful teaching and discussion as well as meaningful worship and relationships.
3. *Opportunity to develop competence.* While this factor was not as strong as the sense of belonging and meaning, youth who felt their skills were being developed through service or leadership opportunities were nonetheless more likely to stay engaged in the youth ministry.[3]

So what can churches do to attract and keep today's youth? One answer is to attend to the above needs. In my interviews with youth, I always asked the question: Why have you stayed in your church, and how does it contribute to your spiritual growth? Anna, a student in a

Christian college, told me that she loves attending her home church because most of her friends are 80 years of age and older. "I don't receive a lot of affirmation from my peers," she says. "Older people are more genuine. They have nothing to lose. When I come to my home church, I am loved, and I love hearing my worth from someone who is older. It's so empowering." Eric, also a college student, remarked, "Sometimes I can get lazy in my faith. Being in a church gives me people who can hold me accountable."

> "The thing that I like most about my congregation is that I feel like I can get involved in anything that I choose to. I don't feel like there are any limitations."
>
> —Scott, 16, *The Lutheran*, September 2005, 17

Sara told me the story about her supportive congregation. "When I was 15, I wanted to learn to play the organ," she explains. "The pastor and people in my church encouraged me. They let me play during services, even though at first I wasn't very good. Playing the organ became my special time with God. Those years showed me how to become closer to God."

> "We must allow ourselves to be awed by the dynamics of their [young adults] souls, not the wrinkle-free complexions of their faces. We must take their wisdom seriously and risk discomfort and uncertainty of transition as we welcome them into our congregations."
>
> —Margaret K. Schwarzer, "Youth's Authority, a Spiritual Revolution," *Gathering the Next Generation*

These young people were affirmed and loved, and they were invited to use their gifts for the congregation. Young people don't want to be ignored. They want to be recognized as valuable members who have ideas and talents to share with the entire church body. Older adults can benefit from the freshness and enthusiasm as well as from the questions of young people, and the adults can be challenged to grow in their own faith. Youth worker Mark Gardner states:

> *As we baptize infants, they become full members of the community and are called to participate fully in the mission of the church according to the gifts God has given them. If we do not honor their baptismal commitment, we miss an*

opportunity to journey with young people as they explore the mystery of God and the power of the Holy Spirit's movement in their lives. We also miss the opportunity to open our own hearts to the work of the Spirit in our lives.

Many churches miss the opportunity to hear what the next generation is saying. They fail to listen to their questions and receive their service. One reason for this reluctance is that youth are historically viewed as inexperienced and unable to minister to others. Nathan Humphrey, editor of *The Next Generation: Essays on the Formation and Ministry of GenX Priests*, says,

> *It hurts to be told by people involved in my process that I don't have any life experience, that I haven't suffered. In my short twenty-five years on this earth, I've had a family member who's attempted suicide, lived with mental illness in my family, seen my parents go bankrupt from helping others, become the child of divorced parents, had a cancer scare. . . . I shouldn't have to prove that I've suffered. Such questions imply that people only begin to feel pain (or learn from it) after thirty, and this disqualifies young people from valid or effective ministry."*[4]

The tragedies of life are not respectful of age. In my interviews with young people, I heard countless stories of suffering, disappointment, and grief. I also heard courageous stories of young people processing tragedy and going on with life. Many of the stories paid tribute to adults who were present to the youth as they worked through their struggles. Older adults can be touched in meaningful ways by the courage of young people, and younger adults need older adults to help them through life's trials. In short, for healthy spiritual and human development, we need each other.

And we need each other to be real. Today's postmodern generations desire authenticity in all of their relationships—including and especially their faith relationships. Boston University chaplain Margaret Schwarzer says,

They [students] are hungry for honest community—the place where they can search for meaning and purpose in their lives, the place of intimacy and welcome where both the vulnerabilities and the sturdy aspects of their humanity are embraced. . . . [T]hey want to belong to a church only if the others in the community are willing to share real doubts, real grief, and real successes. . . . Keeping the spirit alive means stepping into the promise that God is truly present in all the events of our lives."[5]

Young people are looking for examples of lives lived in faith, and many seek those examples in church. But there is an expectation as one enters the door of a church. In my interviews with young people, I often heard the phrase, "I'm looking for a church that feels welcoming." But what is a welcoming church? For Kaela, 13, it was the sense of belonging she felt the minute she stepped into the building. "People of all ages came up to me and introduced themselves to me, and they seemed happy to see me." For Anna, 15, it was the respect and consideration that fellow church members offered. "A welcoming church pays attention to me," she says. "It doesn't ignore me just because I am a teenager."

> "Members of every congregation have to open their hearts and minds as they reach out to a generation of young people who want and need Jesus Christ in their daily lives."
> –Youth Consultation II, www.nbay.ca/consultation.

Both Kaela and Anna belong to a church that intentionally pays attention to its youth. This Episcopal church uses the Rite-13 Liturgy to welcome young people into adolescence. Once a year, when a group of young people moves from childhood to adolescence, a ritual is performed during the Sunday liturgy. The parents and the youth come to the front of the church and make promises to each other—promises that include respect and forgiveness and love. The congregation is asked to support the youth and their parents through the following promises:

PRESIDER: *Will you, their Christian community, support these young people and their parents in this time of change and growth?*

CONGREGATION: We will. We will notice you and include you. We will accept the gifts you bring. We will sing and pray with you. We will challenge you to be generous and compassionate, and to serve Christ at home, at church, and in the world. Will you do the same for us?

"We will notice and include you." Creating a welcoming atmosphere for teens and twentysomethings in a church has to be intentional. How to do this in a specific setting is a journey of exploration. I believe this exploration involves asking questions, conducting visits, and engaging in prayer. The first step is to ask new people in a congregation a series of questions: What draws you to this church? Do you feel welcome? What made you feel welcome? What could we have done to make you more comfortable here?

The second step is to have a group of young and older adults visit other churches and pay attention to how it feels to be a stranger in a church. One congregation tried this exercise. After a number of visits, the wanderers gathered to process what made them feel welcome and what made them feel uncomfortable. A surprising number of visitors felt decidedly ill at ease in the churches they visited. One person observed, "I attended a church, and even went to their adult forum, and not one person talked to me." Another pointed out, "No one talked to me. I felt left out. It felt like the game has been going on for a while and no one invited me in." After the visitors shared their experiences, a time of quiet reflection and prayer followed. This allowed the group to bring their experiences before God and to be attentive to the Holy Spirit's guidance.

YOUTH MINISTRY FOR THE POSTMODERN CHURCH

I cannot discuss mentoring of young people within a church setting without saying some things about youth ministry. Twentieth-century youth ministry began with the purpose of protecting young people from the dangers of society. Youth were encouraged to attend as an alternative to being in places permeated with the dangers of drugs, violence, alcohol, and sex. It was a safe place where youth could have fun and build relationships. Ski trips, hiking, pizza parties, movies, dances, and camping were among the safe activities created for youth. Parents felt comfortable knowing that their adolescent children were being given a safe alternative. Generally speaking, providing activity and entertainment were of primary consideration, while faith development was secondary (I am making a general statement here). There may have been some spiritual development in Bible study, or study of the doctrines of a church (especially in confirmation class), but usually the purpose of the study was to teach the young people how to interpret the Bible and what to believe within the confines of a particular denomination. Young people were rarely given an opportunity to share their own faith stories and ask their own questions.

As the twentieth century waned, fewer teens and young adults attended church. Youth fled after confirmation and, in some churches, confirmation was a ticket *out of* the church rather than a serious recommitment *to* the church. Youth pastors began to examine the content of youth ministry and realized that their charges were looking for something more serious. They were searching for greater depth of Christian experience as well as for the freedom to ask serious questions. "Contemporary music and pizza don't help me with my hard questions," said one young man.

EXEMPLARY YOUTH MINISTRY

A 2004 U.S. study conducted in-depth surveys of 133 congregations representing seven denominations that were known to have consistently developed mature Christian youth. Of the 133 congregations, twenty-one were chosen for intensive weekend site visits. All regions of the United States were represented, and small, medium, and large congregations were included in the mix. Anglo Americans made up a large percentage of the study, but African Americans, Latino Americans, and Asian Americans were also represented.

Four factors stood out as essentials for good youth ministry within a congregation:

- A concrete sense of the presence of a living God who is active among and through the congregation on behalf of the world.
- A pastor (or pastors) who knows, understands, and supports

ministry with youth throughout the life and mission of the congregation.

- A consistent supply of authentic and affirming adults with a transparent faith.

- A network (family, congregational, and peer) of genuine relationships in which young people sense validation and safety, and through which faith seems to be nurtured.[6]

Phrases such as *authentic and affirming adults, transparent faith, genuine relationships, validation,* and *presence of a living God* jumped out at me as I read the results of this survey. In my interviews with youth who are currently members of a church, these qualities emerged repeatedly. Adult members of a church serve as role models to its youth. Young people observe older adults; it's part of their learning experience. And youth especially watch those who serve in ministry. Meggie, 18, appreciated that the

> "If I belong to a church, I need to see people whose lives are changed by religion, who are transformed. I like to hear those stories."
>
> –Anna, 23

adult leaders at her church shared their stories of faith, which helped to guide and support the members of the youth group. Will, 15, appreciated the mutual respect of adults and young people in his congregation.

The plea for a shift in youth ministry isn't just common to the United States. In March 2004, sixty people—youth, adult leaders, and clergy from various parishes—met at St. Mark's Church in St. George, New Brunswick, Canada, to discuss youth ministry in their diocese at Youth Consultation II. The conversation was about the progress made in youth ministry since the previous consultation four years earlier. Although the sixty participants observed real growth, several frustrations remained, including lack of leadership opportunities for young people. As the conference report points out, "[W]e have a feeling that we are sometimes invisible and seen as unimportant by many adults, and that our ideas/opinions are not equal to those of adults. As a result many of us feel we do not belong. Despite a spiritual hunger and a wish to be part of a church family, many of us look elsewhere."[7] The sixty members of Youth Consultation II drafted a list of qualities of a healthy church— a kind of "wish list" for a welcoming parish. They described this welcoming parish as a "family of Christ" that would foster intergenerational relationships and mentoring—a place where adults and youth would work and worship and grow side by side. They saw this type of church as being relevant to people's daily needs as well as being a place of accountability and integrity. This church would encourage its members to reach out to the world at large. It would provide spiritual nurturing for growth in the Christian faith, and it would be a congregation that would welcome all.

A NEW PARADIGM FOR YOUTH MINISTRY

I cite a number of books on the topic of youth ministry in my bibliography, but one organization has had a tremendous influence on today's youth ministry. This organization is Youth Ministry and Spirituality Project, created and funded in 1997 by a Lilly Foundation Grant. Its focus is to integrate Christian spirituality and youth ministry by exploring contemplative prayer, discernment, spiritual direction, community, and Sabbath-living. I invite you to study the table on page 78. It reflects a major paradigm shift for youth ministry in a postmodern society. This paradigm is a spiritual formation model that views youth ministry as more than entertainment. It challenges youth to be formed into the image of Christ. This shift moves away from looking at youth as "blank slates" needing to have information poured into them to a new attitude that views youth as people who already experience God in their lives. The purpose of youth ministry is to affirm those

"Youth ministry should be characterized by silence, solitude, worship, reading, praying, listening, paying attention, and being."

–Mike Yaconelli

experiences of God and to give youth a language to express their knowledge and their questions about God. Churches that believe youth are people who experience God and who, in their own way, thirst for God, have an attitude that draws youth into the life of the congregation and invites them to stay. Those churches value and respect the opinions and ideas of young members.

SPIRITUAL FORMATION MODEL: A COMPARISON		
	The Old Model	**Spiritual Formation Model**
Focus Group	Youth	Youth, youth leaders, congregation
Mission	Knowledge of God involving the mind; answers that stay with youth throughout life.	Intimacy with God (involving mind and heart); practices to encourage this intimacy throughout life.
Conceptual Framework	Youth are blank slates. They need answers about God from adults who know.	Youth are already experiencing God. They need settings to notice, name, and nurture this awareness.
Educational Tools	Lecture, talks, adult Bible studies, games, technology.	Spiritual practices, prayer, service, discussion, spiritual direction, journaling, retreats.
Youth Leader Function	Bearer of God, savior of youth.	Spiritual director—points to the presence of God.
Volunteer Function	Chaperone, help youth leader.	Spiritual mentors, help youth leader and youth discern the movement of God; fellow seekers.
Theology	Faith is accepting a series of statements.	Faith is an ongoing relationship.
Result	Youth ministers burn out; youth leave church; youth and youth ministers alienated from congregation.	Youth ministers grow through youth group; youth have a faith that can grow through life changes; youth, youth ministers, and adults become companions in seeking God.

Used with permission by Mark Yaconelli, Youth Ministry and Spirituality Project.

This spiritual formation model depends on two elements: the use of spiritual practices and a pool of adult spiritual companions.

SPIRITUAL PRACTICES

A couple of weeks after I was hired by Christos Center in 1997, I received a phone call from a Lutheran youth pastor who asked me if I'd heard of something called *lectio divina*. I assured him that I had, and invited him to go on with his story. The kids in his high school youth group heard that their friends in the Episcopal church across town were doing this new prayer, and they wanted him to teach it to them. The pastor asked me if there was a course in *lectio divina* that he could take or a book he could read. I gave him a Web page with a simple explanation of *lectio divina* and strongly urged him to practice the prayer in his own prayer time. I reminded him that *lectio divina* was a way to pray the scriptures, and it was a prayer that needed to be practiced before teaching it to somebody else. I assured him that after a few weeks he'd be able to model this prayer for his youth group. Furthermore, I told him that *lectio divina* and other spiritual practices such as centering prayer, silence, pilgrimage, and spiritual direction aren't new to the Christian church. Finally, I stressed that there's no minimum age for the practice of these disciplines. Unfortunately, I didn't follow up on our conversation, but I hope this young man listened to the young people he was working with and shared the richness of a variety of spiritual practices with them.

While I've written about spiritual disciplines in previous chapters, I want to emphasize that these practices can be offered within the context of a church. A number of youth workers shared with me that they've begun to use quieter prayer forms with their youth, including a small room or chapel, dimmed lights, candles, a sacred image (cross, icon, a photograph or painting, rocks, twigs, shells, tree bark). The prayer experience often begins with a scripture reading or a short paragraph from a Christian book, followed by a time of silence, then sometimes a Taizé song or other short song followed by more silence. The prayer experience usually ends with verbal intercessory prayer and an invitation to share how God was present in the experience. One youth worker shared with me that he was hesitant to try this with his "rowdy" group, so before they entered the quiet room for the first time, he explained the history of spiritual practices, talked about sacred space and the value of silence, and invited them just to try it. Without asking his group to do this, they spontaneously took off their shoes before they entered the holy place. This voluntary act set a tone, and while the group remained "rowdy" in other places, they were, without exception, respectful and quiet when they entered their holy place.

The simplicity of the holy place creates an atmosphere very different from the noisy world outside, and it allows youth to center on God. In my interviews with members and leaders of youth groups, the element of simplicity emerged above all others. People who work with youth as well as youth themselves clearly stated that program-driven, highly structured, entertainment-oriented youth ministry just doesn't bring young people the depth they desire. Today's teens and twentysomethings want to see God in church, at youth group, and in everyday life. They want to know that it's okay to pray anywhere, at any time.

Helping young people see God's presence in everyday life is a goal many youth pastors share with me. Pastor Chris Berthelsen of Stillwater, Minnesota, took her junior high youth group on a service project—raking leaves in various yards of older members of the congregation. At dusk after the last yard was raked, Chris invited the weary youth to lie down in the yard and be quiet for a few minutes. Each gladly complied and watched the stars emerge in the darkening sky. Chris remembers, "During those moments of silence on the cool lawn, God was so present that each of us could almost reach up and touch the Presence. Those young people openly talked about that evening for months." There was no program and no agenda for that day except to help some people and then to rest, gaze at the stars, and let God be God.

No Program, No Agenda, No Cost

In my research, I observed several youth ministry programs, and those doing exemplary youth work, who didn't rely on established curricula or materials. Youth ministry curricula are often costly and highly programmatic, and many of the curricula are concerned with numbers, success, marketing, technology, and entertainment. While some of the ideas offered in a curriculum may be valuable, much of youth ministry needs to rely on the uniqueness of the group, the situation, the adult leaders, and the Holy Spirit. Youth Ministry and Spirituality Project founder Mark Yaconnelli says,

> *Today's popular youth ministry models are creative, dynamic, and fun. Yet something's missing. In a typical youth group, how many kids actually encounter the resurrected Christ? Does our focus on youth directors, curricula, and programs crowd out opportunities for kids to experience God? I think a youth program is effective only when it offers kids the space, tools, and time to encounter God's transforming love.*[8]

One youth pastor experimented with Yanconelli's idea by providing space for her high school youth to encounter God. Rather than relying on a youth-group manual for her meetings, she gathered all her adult volunteers an hour before youth group. The majority of the hour was spent in prayer—asking the question, "What are we called to tonight?" From that prayer came the focus of the evening's events. After the hour of prayer and the youth arrived, the young people and the adults always began the meeting with a check-in: "Where have you experienced God since we last met?" "What's been hard for you this week?" "What has been a joy?" The group was encouraged to listen carefully to one another. After check-in, a prayer experience was introduced. Often it was *lectio divina*, a centering prayer, or some Taizé chants. This was followed by a time of silence and then sharing about the experience. After the prayer, the adults presented what they heard in prayer prior to the meeting. Sometimes those ideas were acted on; sometimes not. "Not having a book or a program to follow was risky," admitted the pastor,

> *but God always gave us ideas. Sometimes the idea was to let the youth plan the evening. We always had stuff around, art supplies, bibles, food, and access to the Internet. One time, we researched and made individual labyrinths. One time I threw out the question, "How do you know you are dating the right person?" Once we had skit night—paper bags of*

props and each group illustrated a gospel story using the props.
Another time we brainstormed ways to collect food for a local
food pantry.

This youth pastor understood the value of prayer in ministry. She relied on the guidance of the Holy Spirit rather than on programs or the opinions of others. She understood that her ministry with youth was God's ministry, but it took courage to do what she did. Conducting youth ministry without the prop of a curriculum is radical. She took some criticism and was not always sure what to do, but she stayed true to her own prayer times, regularly met with her spiritual director, and relied on prayer and discernment from her group of adult volunteers.

Conducting youth ministry this way is a radical approach in today's church. But it's an approach with a foundation in prayer. I believe that all ministry needs to be led by the Holy Spirit. I believe that the number of hours spent on planning youth events needs to be fewer than the number of hours spent in prayer—both individual prayer of the ministers and the adult volunteers and communal prayer of the youth, the youth ministry team, and the congregation. (An excellent resource for making prayer a priority in youth ministry is *Contemplative Youth Ministry: Practicing the Presence of Jesus* by Mark Yaconelli. See the reference on page 128.)

CHURCH SERVICES THAT APPEAL TO TODAY'S YOUTH AND YOUNG ADULTS

LITURGICAL SERVICE

Liturgy has all the elements of spiritual discipline: ritual, prayer, silence, scripture, music, communion, confession, tradition, and community. Liturgical ritual and rhythm appeal to postmodern spirituality through the use of experience, participation, images, and connection. It's no wonder many young people today are drawn to churches that have traditional liturgy, and it's not a surprise that non-liturgical churches are exploring the use of ritual in their services. I encourage members of liturgical denominations to ready themselves to welcome new people who haven't had liturgy in their past, but who hunger for it. And I encourage members of non-liturgical churches to pay attention to the need for ritual in their services. Robert Webber, director of the Institute of Worship Studies at Northern Baptist Seminary in Lombard, Illinois, observes, "What is happening in the religion of teenagers is nothing short of astounding. They want to return to a more stable time, a period of tradition. Not the tradition of the fifties, but of a much earlier time, the tradition of the old, very old times."

Webber continues with this youth director's statement: "What appeals to this new generation is the cathedral and stained-glass window. Take the pews out, let them sit on the floor, burn incense, have Scripture readings, lots of music, chants even, and have communion, and they say "Wow, this is me."[9]

Kami Rice began attending an Episcopal church when she was in her twenties. At first, she was reluctant. She didn't expect much from a "dead liturgy" and "reciting someone else's words." But what she found was "a church body alive with the presence of God at work. I loved the integrated, participatory feel of the gathering and loved the music spread out throughout the service. I loved feeling connected to my fellow worshippers in an act of corporate worship, rather than being an individual worshipping in the midst of a crowd."[10] Kami found a church home where a living God is worshipped with a liturgy, rooted in centuries of tradition. The concept of tradition is important to this generation of young people, who feel comfortable with something that's survived the test of time. Kami continues, "There is something in these practices and remembrances that I feel may hold some key to the deeper faith experience I'm longing for these days. There's a beauty in knowing that this faith I'm pursuing is not something that just emerged yesterday. Instead, it's a relationship people have been participating in for thousands of years."[11]

> "The church always goes wrong when it tries to appear cool. It never goes wrong when it tries to attend to people's deepest thirst."
>
> —Judy Tarjanyi quoting Tom Beaudoin, "Gen-X Christians Want Their Churches to Be Spiritual, Not Hip," *Toledo Blade*, May 25, 2000

Earlier in this book, I discussed Leonard Sweet's acronym, EPIC. Today's youth want to experience God. They desire to participate in the life of the church, and they value images, symbols, mystery, and community. When one enters a liturgical church with symbols, candles, and silence, one is entering a sacred place—a place alive with mysterious presence. All of this appeals to the postmodern mind and heart.

A word of caution, however: Turning down the lights and using a few candles is not the essence of the new way of drawing young people to church. Nor is participating in liturgy the only way one encounters the living God. The key to drawing people to church is prayer and listening to the guidance of the Holy Spirit. Church leaders who wish to welcome young people into their community need to pray and reflect on their own unique style. They need to ponder questions such as: How does God want us to be? What are our unique gifts? What are young people in our community looking for? How do we need to grow and change to be a welcoming community to youth? It is not uncommon to have ministers and lay people pray for a year or two before they even begin a ministry with youth or before they reconstruct a previous one.

Being a welcoming community for youth and young adults may not look like candles and icons. Rather, it might be like the church Mark Yaconelli describes in *Contemplative Youth Ministry*. The story begins with an Episcopal priest and his wife in a small church in a Colorado ski town who wanted to welcome young people. Their first step was to pray. After a year of weekly prayer and discernment with eight other adults, the word "home" kept emerging. Soon the church was providing meals and warm clothing to young people who had no home and who drifted from town to town. Their ministry became "Grandma's Home Cooking. Fresh-made soup. Home baked cookies. Free shoes, jackets, and pants. A listening ear."[12] This story of a small church in Colorado teaches us that what is essential to providing a community for young people is listening for the Spirit's guidance and asking: What is God's direction for this church, and how can we be a community where young people feel loved and welcomed, and not judged? How can we be a place where all of our members share the presence of Christ in our lives and who grow in that Presence?

POSTMODERN AND EMERGENT CHURCH SERVICES
I entered the sanctuary on a late Saturday afternoon. Chairs were

scattered around the space in random order. Some people sat in chairs; others sat on the floor. In the middle of the space was a small water fountain surrounded by about fifty pairs of shoes—fancy dress shoes, work boots, slippers, athletic shoes, and children's shoes. The lights were dim—with candles randomly placed in the back of the sanctuary. There were about sixty of us in attendance, including people in their twenties, families with small children, teens, and older folks. A young man welcomed us and explained the order of service. We sang a few songs—mostly softer contemporary Christian songs. We were asked to reflect in small groups on a film that focused on living life in a community. The question for discussion was: Why would we like or not like to enter into the community presented in that film? Judy, the adult leader, gave a talk on the value of community and the different roles people have in a communal setting. There was more singing, again soft music, accompanied by a few instruments. Then Dan, another adult leader, led a prayer experience. He asked seven children, sitting on the floor in front of him, to give each person in the room a shoe. Dan asked us to imagine the kind of person who would wear that shoe, and we were instructed to pray for that person. The prayer ended with an invitation to light a candle and place it in the middle of the room near the fountain. Silence was maintained during this prayer experience while people moved in random order to light their candles. The evening ended with prayer for a family, members of the congregation, who were going to China to teach. Conversation and refreshments followed.[13]

The following Sunday evening, I enjoyed another postmodern/ emergent church service. This time the service was in a mid-sized room with chairs and couches and about forty candles resting on draped fabric. I received a warm welcome as people introduced themselves to me. Soft music was being played as pictures of nature scenes were projected on a screen. There were about thirty people in the room—mostly in their twenties, with a smattering of older folks. We began with a number of songs: some were short, repetitive, Taizé-style songs, and others were traditional hymns accompanied by guitar. We were invited to reflect on a scripture passage and to share our reflections with the group. It was Mother's Day, so Andrew Miller, the worship leader, introduced his mom, who read the children's book *The Runaway Bunny* and related it to how God loves us. A man gave a short teaching about the early church in the Acts of the Apostles. Lorinda, the youth leader, gave a conversational sermon, followed by more music, time for quiet prayer, and the opportunity to go to a prayer station to receive prayer from others.[14]

The terms *postmodern* and *emergent* are used today to describe these types of services. They are services that emerge from the prayer and discussion of a core group of people. There is no set formula. Every service is different, and every service comes out of the prayer of the core group. Emergent services "create a sense of community in which God reaches out to others, and together we learn the art of living in the ways of Jesus," observes Andrew Miller, 20, worship leader.

From participating in services like these, as well as others—both on the Web and in person—I've devised a list of elements often included in these new Christian services.

- *A sacred atmosphere*: There is an atmosphere of quiet sacredness—usually manifested by candles, sacred objects (crosses, icons, colorful fabric), natural objects (rocks, shells, water); and visual images of natural beauty or sacred places or people engaged in helping others.

- *Informality*: These services are not usually held in a sanctuary unless the sanctuary can be cleared of chairs. Usually a plain room or a chapel are used. Chairs are randomly placed, or people sit on the floor. No one dresses up. A group of people preside rather than a single priest or pastor. Most of the presiders are young lay people. Rather than a set ritual, each service is different.

- *Intergenerational*: People of all ages plan and attend these services and look to each other for wisdom.

- *Experiential*: The service includes experiences and movement. People move around to light candles, to go to prayer spaces, to converse in a group. People are invited to see, to touch, to smell, to taste, to hear.

- *Hospitality*: Usually these services are small, so hospitality is easy to facilitate. New people are greeted. People circulate and introduce themselves. Sometimes nametags are used, and usually

snacks are available before, during, and after the service.
- *Music*: Songs are contemporary Christian, but soft contemporary—not rock. Instruments are guitars, bass, and piano. Taizé-style music is often used—or lyrics that are short, simple, and repeated often. And hymns are sung, but are accompanied by more contemporary instruments. Sometimes Native American, Celtic, and African American songs and prayer are used.
- *Inclusion*: It is clear that everyone is welcome and respected
- *Story*: Stories are read and told. The gospel stories of Jesus' life are most often used. Sermons are a series of stories, and people share stories with each other.
- *Teaching*: Sometimes there is a teaching on a topic. Those who orchestrate these kinds of services know that those who are unchurched or nominally churched attend, so it's appropriate to do some teaching on basic Christianity.
- *Sermons*: Sermons are informal, concrete, and practical; sometimes visual. Usually the people take something practical into their daily lives from the sermon. Sometimes the participants are encouraged to contribute to the sermon, and often the sermons are discussions.
- *Prayer*: Prayer is taken seriously, and a variety of prayers are practiced: petition, intercession, prayer with scripture, centering prayer, Christian meditation, and breath prayer. Sometimes spiritual practices are taught. People are taught *lectio divina* or are taught to keep a journal. Worship leader Andrew Miller, 20, observes, "It's important to adhere to the spiritual disciplines that are ancient in origin in such a way that people my age can relate to them."
- *Pop culture*: These services recognize the role of popular culture in people's lives. For example, an excerpt of a film might be viewed and discussed.

Why do these types of worship services work with today's youth and with youth-minded individuals? In short, they're welcoming, informal, sacred, practical, experiential, intergenerational, prayerful, and community building.

While liturgical and emergent services appeal to a growing number of young people today, contemporary worship services are offered in many churches. These services are centered on contemporary music, which tends to be lively and loud. Participants are invited to sing and to clap their hands. Songs are followed by a message or a sermon or faith sharing, followed by more singing. The worship service ends with prayers and more songs. While contemporary services have been the norm for many years, the young people I interviewed are growing weary of these services and are looking for something quieter, something involving ritual, something with more meat and authenticity in the message. Many young people are searching for ways to change the way they look at God and at society. Some churches are recognizing this shift and are adopting elements of ritual and depth into their contemporary style.

TODAY'S INTERGENERATIONAL CHURCH

Look again at the spiritual formation table on page 78 and observe that the new spiritual formation paradigm is dependent on spiritual mentors. Also, recall one of the needs discovered in the Exemplary Youth Ministry study: "A consistent supply of authentic and affirming adults with a transparent faith." Part of this is not new. Church ministry to young people has always included adult involvement. What is new is the role adults now play in this ministry. In the old paradigm, the youth pastor was the leader who brought God to the youth—kind of like the Pied Piper, leading adolescents away from the dangers of society by providing alternative entertainment and, as an aside, mentioning God. (I am generalizing, of course.) The new paradigm invites the youth pastor and other adults of the parish to journey with young people by being transparent in their own faith. Each generation has the privilege of forming the next generation's faith development and, if there is mutual sharing, both the new and the older generations

> "We know that our young people can't catch the faith without being around people of mature faith. Those who have it need to be hanging out with those who are still on the quest."
> —Peggy Contos, bishop's assistant, Golf Coast Lutheran Synod, from *The Lutheran*, September 2005, 16.

are blessed. "Having adult leaders helps me understand myself on multiple levels," says Kirk, 14. "Our adult leaders serve as our guides." This mutuality between young and not so young has a fancy name in today's Christian milieu—intergenerational ministry.

Intergenerational ministry pairs young and old in similar situations—teens and 60-year-olds, for example, working together framing a house for Habitat for Humanity. Space is created so both can tell their stories, and both grow.

Young people want to believe that Someone loves them and hears their cry. They want someone to listen to their stories. Adults in a congregation can affirm that God does love them and desires to be a part of their lives.

SPIRITUAL DIRECTION IN A CHURCH SETTING

I cannot complete this chapter without again stressing the importance of spiritual companionship for today's young seekers. Spiritual direction or companionship can and must be available to people in churches. In chapter three, I shared examples of group direction being offered in congregations. In recent years, youth pastors have gone through the spiritual direction preparation program at Christos Center because they believe that an important part of their role as youth leaders is to function as spiritual directors. They need to ask spiritual direction-type questions that will aid youth in their own faith development. Many youth workers admitted to me that they do informal spiritual direction all the time: before the Sunday service or during a break while serving at a food pantry. One youth director named it "three-minute theology," doing spiritual direction on the run. Young people think of questions spontaneously and want to be heard now. Trained youth directors as well as adult volunteers can serve as spiritual directors for young people in a church setting. Look for more about equipping adults to accompany young people in chapter six.

SPIRITUAL DIRECTION FOR CHURCH-SPONSORED PILGRIMAGE AND MISSION TRIPS

"The first time in my life I ever actually felt the presence of God was on pilgrimage," says Meggie, 18. "It was a hot day. I was cranky and uncomfortable. We walked to St. Brigid's Well [in Ireland], took hands, and said the Lord's Prayer together. Just at that moment, a cool breeze came over us. It was God."

In the last two decades, every two or three years, hundreds of thousands of Roman Catholic young adults have taken a pilgrimage to places such as Cologne, Germany, Toronto, and Rome for World Youth Day. Why? For one 17-year-old girl it's "an opportunity to discover my faith for myself instead of just having it handed to me."[15] Pilgrimage attendee Rev. William Baer adds, "They [young people] want more than endless computer games and music. Instead of living vicariously through the media, they want to do something real, to be accountable. . . . The pilgrimage to World Youth Day is a rite of passage in the most profound sense of the word."[16]

Pilgrimage and mission trips can be a rite of passage, with the potential of bringing the presence of God into the hearts of youth. But young people going on pilgrimage and mission trips need to be carefully prepared and mentored, and particular attention must be paid to spiritual preparation. I cannot stress this enough. In fact, I suspect that no one, young or old, is adequately spiritually prepared to go on pilgrimage or on mission trips. (But that's a topic for another book.) In her article "Youth's Authority," Margaret Schwarzer, chaplain at Boston University, observes:

> *Pilgrimages . . . give these young Christians the opportunity to be consciously open to transforming grace. Working in soup kitchens or homeless shelters, participating in unusual worship services, building houses . . . all such experiences engage them because they are both acting out their faith and living into the new possibilities their faith creates for them. Generation X is committed to acting in the world, but they want to be grounded in a spiritual understanding of the work before they act. They want to know where they are standing before they move into new spiritual territory. So they look inward before they turn outward to pastoral actions or actions of social justice.*[17]

In the turning-inward process, youth look to adult mentors—those who have turned inward and then have used their gifts for the greater good. As young people are prepared for mission or pilgrimage, adult mentors start the preparation process by creating a community. Youth and their adult companions rely on each other as they travel to distant places, so before they leave they need to have a bond that will provide the strength needed for the coming journey. Activities that encourage this community include frequent meetings before the journey, fund-raising projects, camping trips that teach how to live in close quarters, and times of communal prayer.

Deb Gardner, an adult mission-trip leader who has prepared several groups for ministry, says that honest conversation before the journey helps to form community. She uses a series of questions, including: What are you looking forward to? What fears do you have about going? What insights do you expect to gain? What gifts can you offer this community on this mission trip? Deb says that it's important to remain available to the group throughout the trip. When young people are out of their home territory, they seem freer to talk, to reflect, and to ask questions. They see people in poverty and they are prompted to ask the big questions of life, so they look to their adult companions for guidance.

Faye, an adult youth leader in a Minneapolis suburban church who accompanied youth on a mission trip to Romania, observed that everyone has culture shock while on mission trip—no one can ever be fully prepared to see the poverty and violence of another culture. She stresses the importance of the presence of caring and alert adults. While in Romania, she carefully watched each of the youth, and gently made herself available to those who were having a hard time with the experience.

Prayer also helps build community, and it gives young Christians the spiritual strength to do a mission trip or a pilgrimage. One mission group had prayer partners during the preparation time as well as during the trip. Church members usually promise to pray for those on missions or pilgrimages. Establishing simple prayer experiences such as breath prayer or centering prayer for the pilgrims before the trip enables them to continue those experiences when they are far from home. Lizzie, 17, who attended a pilgrimage to the Celtic Center in Ireland in 2003, summarized her experience:

There is no way to be fully prepared for pilgrimage. Just go and do it. Be ready for surprises. Have an open mind and open heart because the experience will surprise you. So much went wrong with our pilgrimage—delayed flights, getting lost—but that made the experience better. That became part of the pilgrimage, part of the struggle. It was very helpful to know our group, to have caring adult leaders, to all be on the same page, and to love being together.

> "What I find people my age thirsting for makes me feel intensely expectant of God bringing another renewal of the church in my generation. I want to be a part of it. I feel blessed to be alive at this time in history with all the wisdom of so many ages to draw upon and while a tide is turning."
>
> —Mary, 30

WRAP-UP

Reaching out to youth within a church setting includes balance. It's important to invite young people to contribute to the life of the church, and it's crucial to take the faith life of youth seriously and provide opportunities for faith development. A church that's serious about its young people needs to invite storytelling in which both young and old are encouraged to share their stories. And it's essential to have fun. Periodic camping trips, pizza parties, movie nights, and intergenerational parties—all contribute to healthy parish life. Healthy church life is happening, and I feel passionately hopeful about this next generation of Christians who will lead the church—especially if those of us who are passing the life of faith on to them do it with love, respect, and attention to God. Episcopal priest Richard Kew says what's in my heart:

> *If members of my generation are to be responsible stewards of these next few years, it is imperative that we do our best to identify, nurture, support, mentor, and set loose for service a new, young, and dynamic generation of leaders. As I look at the world today, in some respects, I wish I were younger. The years ahead will not be easy. They will be fast-moving, exciting, sometimes excruciating, but overflowing with a totally different set of opportunities to know Christ—and to make Christ known.*[18]

NOTES

1. Robert A. Ludwig, *Reconstructing Catholicism for a New Generation* (New York: Crossroad, 1996), 25.

2. Ibid., 28.

3. Kara Powell, "What Attracts and Keeps Students at Your Church?," *Youthworker Journal*, www.youthspecialties.com/articles/topics/getting results.

4. Nathan Humphrey, "Trusting the Process," in *Gathering the Next Generation: Essays on the Formation and Ministry of GenX Priests*, ed. Nathan Humphrey (Harrisburg, PA: Morehouse Publishing, 2000), 27.

5. Margaret Schwarzer, "Youth's Authority," in *Gathering the Next Generation*, 59.

6. *The Study of Exemplary Congregations in Youth Ministry*, www.exemplarym.com/sept04.

7. See www.nbay.ca/consultation.

8. "Ancient-Future Youth Ministry," *Group Magazine*, www.ymsp.org/resources.

9. Uwe Siemon-Netto, "Faith: New Generation Is Looking Back," www.issuesetc.org/resource/archive, 1.

10. Kami Rice, "Of Advent and Other Seasons," *Method X*, www.methodx.net/articles/columns.

11. Ibid.

12. Mark Yaconelli, *Contemplative Youth Ministry: Practicing the Presence of Jesus* (Grand Rapids, MI: Zondervan, 2006), 17–76.

13. Oasis, a Ministry of Hope Church, Oakdale, Minnesota, www.hopechurchoakdale.com.

14. Presbyterian Church of the Master, Coon Rapids, Minnesota.

15. Katherine Kersten, "For Youth, Pilgrimage Is Rite of Passage," *Minneapolis Star Tribune*, August, 15, 2005, B1.

16. Ibid., B5.

17. Margaret K. Schwarzer, "Youth's Authority: A Spiritual Revolution," in *Gathering the Next Generation*, 61.

18. Richard Kew, "Tomorrow's World, Tomorrow's Church, Tomorrow's Leaders," in *Gathering the Next Generation*, 11.

CHAPTER FIVE

MENTORING SPECIAL GROUPS

So far we've looked at teens and twentysomethings as a combined group. In this chapter, let's examine several unique and specific subgroups of young people: youth workers, seminarians, high school students, post-secondary school students, and older adults whose lives are impacted by youth.

MENTORING CHURCH YOUTH WORKERS

A number of years ago, I received a phone call from Nate, a 29-year-old youth pastor in his first ministry position. After he realized that I'd calmly listen to him, his end of the conversation went something like this:

> *For as long as I could remember, I wanted to be a pastor. I've been here in this church for six months, and now I'm not sure I made the right choice. Maybe I'm wrong, but it seems like this congregation wants me to work some kind of miracle. I am in charge of the middle school youth group, the high school youth group, the confirmation class, and the young adult group; but there is practically no one in the young adult group. They all leave after confirmation. I have the impression this church wants me to make good Lutherans out*

of all these kids and to bring back the ones who have left. But practically no one on staff or from the congregation wants to help me. I've never felt so alone in my life.

Unfortunately, Nate's story is not unique among parish youth ministers.

One of the most influential books I discovered in my search for literature on youth ministry is *The Godbearing Life: The Art of Soul Tending for Youth Ministry* by Kenda Creasy Dean and Ron Foster. The authors refer to youth ministry as bearing the light of Christ into the lives of youth. But as I heard stories like Nate's, I learned that bearing the light of Christ is grueling work, and the work often extinguishes the light of the workers themselves.

So what exactly is it that dampens the energy and enthusiasm of youth workers? I interviewed a group of parish youth workers who had gathered for a seminar on youth and young adult ministry in St. Paul, Minnesota. During a break, I entered into a lively conversation with the participants, whose experience level ranged from a few months to three years. I asked the group to tell me how they fill their day—what they do when they wake up, when they're at work, and when they head back home. Their answers included paperwork, staff meetings, program and event set up, volunteer recruitment, and budgetary decisions. They also talked about spending time in conversations with parents, or defending decisions they've made. Finally, near the end of the list, they talked about their relationships with youth. They all expressed a frustration at not having enough time to work with the young people. Throughout this conversation, I noticed that none of them talked about their personal lives outside of work. None of them mentioned caring for themselves, and none of them mentioned personal attention to spiritual matters. So I directly asked the question: What do you do to take care of yourself? Most of the answers focused on social events with friends. The young man who had been in youth ministry for three years mentioned taking time alone to go skiing. Finally, I asked what they do to attend to their own spiritual growth. A few mentioned that they read the Bible sometimes or pray a little. One admitted that he'd like to have a spiritual director, but his church told him they couldn't afford it.

BURNOUT

Veteran youth ministers state that the major reason youth workers burn out—typically after only eighteen months—is that they don't attend to their personal spiritual life. They yield to the pressures placed on them by church staff and parents, and those pressures deplete their energy. They don't have the strength and the holy guidance that a life of paying attention to God could give them, and they don't have a spiritual community for their own needs. Typically, the only spiritual community they have is the one for whom they work. Having their own faith community and having spiritual direction is countercultural to many Christian church staffs—not just youth workers.

In *The Godbearing Life*, Kenda Creasy Dean and Ron Foster call this lack of attention to prayer and personal spiritual life, "scrawny faith." It's difficult to be engaged in Christian ministry when you're not being filled by God's grace. Moreover, it's inauthentic for youth pastors to lead youth in a relationship with God when they can't nurture their own relationship. "We question the integrity of sharing scrawny faith with teenagers who know the difference between Chicken McNuggets and a full-course meal and who are starved for the latter," says Dean.[1]

Let me to tell you the story of a Lutheran pastor who did something about his "scrawny faith." He decided to go into the sanctuary from 12:30 to 1:00 p.m. every day to pray. People who phoned the office were told: "Pastor is praying. He'll call you back." Pastor is praying—what a comforting thought. And what a model for that church! Within months, the church council followed his example and decided to become a praying council. They learned more about prayer—about prayer, not just about *saying* prayers. They began their meetings with a twenty-minute period of prayer that included time for silence. When faced with a major decision or a disagreement, the head of the council stopped the proceedings and invited everyone to be in silent prayer. Without being aware of it, they shifted their role from a governing council to a discerning council. Next, the church staff took the baton. They decided to go on retreat so they could become a more cohesive group. They, too, learned to pray together while on retreat, and brought prayer practices back to their daily setting. What was the outcome? More cooperation between staff members. More discernment regarding decisions, and less staff burnout.

Cooperation and discernment are valuable assets for church workers, especially those who work with youth. So how can a spiritual director minister in such a way that the youth pastor's spiritual needs are met? A spiritual companion can recognize that youth workers are active, busy people who have zeal, energy, and passion. But they're asked by the congregation to deal with those considered to be the church's most challenging members—teens and young adults. Often these youth workers aren't spiritually and emotionally supported by their church staff or church members. In fact, sometimes they're taken advantage of, criticized, and blamed. Stories of clergy abuse have appeared in the press—and it does exist—but I've seen many instances of abuse *of* the clergy and church staff. It doesn't take long for a youth pastor to become disillusioned and to lose energy, zeal, a sense of call, and even faith.

However, a spiritual director, a spiritual companion, or a mentor can offer gentle guidance, care, and affirmation. A companion can focus attention on youth workers and listen to their stories. When I work with youth ministers, they often begin by talking about their personal lives—their dating relationships, living situations, car payments, and chronic fatigue. Youth workers' lives in ministry are focused on listening to others' problems all the time, but no one listens to them. When I sit with youth workers for the first time, it's like a dam has burst and everything they've wanted to say for months comes pouring out. So I listen and I affirm.

Spiritual companionship is a lifeline for people in youth ministry. It allows them to look at the chaos of their lives and prompts them to slow down. One youth pastor came into direction because he recognized how frantic his life had become. He noticed that he was always busy doing something, so in spiritual direction he sought ways to slow down and just be. Another came to spiritual direction because: "If I'm not taking my own breaks of rest and prayer,

> "[A]ll of us who engage in youth ministry should be under the care of a spiritual director, at least for a time. . . . Direction helps us grow in faith, stay committed to our disciplines, and gives us a few hours a month to be quiet and listen for God's voice in the voice of another."
>
> —Tony Jones, *Soul Shaper*, 127.

I get sucked into this busy vortex of ministry, and it changes what I do and who I am. My spiritual director reminds me to take those breaks."

YOUTH WORKERS AND PRAYER

A spiritual director/companion can encourage youth workers to balance *being* with *doing, prayer* with *action*, through caring for their own spiritual, physical, and psychological needs. Youth workers need to be invited to be present to the mystery of God in their own situations and in their work. They need to be encouraged to take some time every day to be intentional in their communication with God.

Much of what I do as a spiritual director is to enable people to discover their own style of being in God's presence. Classical spiritual disciplines such as scripture meditation, centering prayer, and devotional reading appeal to some, while others like to use images such as pictures, personal sacred objects, or symbols. Many seek the presence of God through recreational activity: hiking, fishing, skiing, climbing, and biking. Still others invite the presence of God through music or thorough body movement, sacred dance, the labyrinth, or meditative walking. A spiritual director can teach some of these prayer types and invite directees to experiment with them.

One prayer method I recommend to people in ministry and to those preparing for ministry is a method taught by St. Ignatius of Loyola. This prayer involves using your imagination to place yourself in a gospel story. When I teach this method in a spiritual direction session, I invite my directee to choose a story, and I read it slowly. Sometimes I choose a Gospel story. During the second reading, I invite the directee to use her imagination to place herself in the story as an observer, paying attention to the sights, sounds, and smells. The story of Jesus welcoming the children is a good one for those not familiar with this prayer method. I encourage the directee to visualize the setting, to watch the people, and to notice the noises and even the smells. I invite her to watch Jesus, to hear him gently speak to the children, to watch him as he holds children in his lap. Sometimes, if a directees is ready, I'll invite her to look into Jesus' eyes and experience his love—or maybe even talk to him. Then we spend some time in silence, and if the directee is willing, we may discuss the experience. Whether directees use this way of prayer during a spiritual direction session or in their own prayer time, many have reported profound encounters with Jesus. This method of praying connects youth workers with the ministry of Jesus, and it has the potential to enable them to experience the intense love of Christ.

Because the life of a youth minister is so busy, another prayer I like to teach is breath prayer. I invite directees to sit in a comfortable position and I ask them to take a deep breath—in slowly and out slowly. With an inward breath, I encourage them to invite God's peace or Jesus' love. With an outward breath, I invite them to let go of frustration, anger, and worry. Regular practice with this kind of prayer allows directees to return to it anytime: in the car, while in a meeting, or even while working with a young person.

While breath prayer is useful at any time of the day, it's important to encourage directees to go away for extended times to rest, recreate, and pray. I find that it's best to invite directees to choose their own way. For some, it may be going on a ski trip (without the youth group!), or a bike or hiking trip. Some need to go to a retreat center and be alone in the silence. Others need to connect with people who can nurture them in special ways.

In my interviews with youth ministers, I was pleasantly surprised to hear how many regularly worship outside their own workplace congregation. One youth minister told me, "I try to worship somewhere else about two or three times a month, in a community where I'm not responsible and where no one knows me." Being an anonymous face in a worshiping community allows the freedom to be relaxed, not "on call," and to invite the presence of God. Others actually belong to a community outside the one for which they work, and they invite that community to minister to them. As a spiritual director, I can ask directees if they might consider joining a worship community or a para-church organization unconnected to their workplace.

YOUTH WORKERS AND RELATIONSHIPS

I've found that it's crucial for youth workers to be in a healthy relationship with their senior pastor or rector as well as with other staff members. Often I hear loneliness in the voices of my youth minister directees. Some feel that youth ministry is shoved to the back corner of the church's agenda. Others feel that the senior pastor and staff consider youth ministry a low priority. Sometimes I ask:

- I hear loneliness in your voice. Is this true?
- Where is the loneliness coming from?
- How often do you meet with your supervising pastor?
- Do you feel free to talk to him like you talk to me?
- Do you pray together?
- Does that person affirm you?
- How do you relate to the other members of the church staff?
- Do you feel supported by them?

Sometimes the loneliness comes from a lack of a life outside the church. This is especially true of single youth workers. It's important that parish youth ministers connect with people their own age or older. If youth pastors don't have a few relationships outside their church, they might develop a "need to be needed" mentality. A spiritual director is aware that a desire to be needed can turn into unhealthy relationships with youth, and the director can invite youth workers to probe their motivations. I ask questions such as:

- Do you find yourself consistently giving up your personal time to attend to the needs of one of your youth?
- Do you think about your ministry a lot when you are not at church?
- Do you fanaticize about anyone in your youth group?
- When you are praying for your youth group, can you finish the prayer and trust that God will hold that situation?
- On a scale of one to ten, how detached do you think you are from your ministry?

Finally, a spiritual director/companion to youth workers can remind them that they're never alone. The spiritual director can point directees to the life and ministry of Jesus and invite them to look to Jesus for companionship.

MENTORING HIGH SCHOOL STUDENTS

When my husband and I were parenting our daughters during the 1980s and 1990s, I spent hours poring over books on the stages of toddlerhood, the preschool years, and the golden age of grade school. But when our daughters entered the teen years, I discovered an information void and soon realized there was a reason: No one could write on teenagers because no one had a clue about how they thought and functioned. What further contributed to my frustration was that I taught high school for ten years and had a few graduate courses on adolescent psychology under my belt, and I still didn't have a clue. As we raised our daughters, the emotions, attitudes, and behaviors kept changing—sometimes from hour to hour.

I do love teens (especially now that mine have grown into fine adult women). I love their enthusiasm and their passion. But how are we to nurture them? And what are they looking for? And how, in God's name, do we help them with faith? I've touched on a few ideas in previous chapters. Teens need freedom to explore, to question, and to stretch, but they do need boundaries. They need to feel welcomed by a faith community, and it is important that they be empowered to do ministry. Adolescents need older adults to listen to them and to model what it means to be a Christian man or woman. They need faith formation relevant to their daily lives, and they desire more than words—far more. They want concrete experience. They want to touch, feel, and sense God's presence in their daily lives. They need to be enabled to connect with God and to feel God's love. Finally, as adolescents transition from childhood to adulthood, they need the assurance and affirmation of all kinds of adults: parents, teachers, coaches, employers, church staff, and church members.

> "Adolescents are looking for a soul-shaking, heart-waking, world-changing God to fall in love with; and if they do not find that God in the Christian church, they will most certainly settle for lesser gods elsewhere."
> —Kenda Creasy Dean and Ron Foster, Introduction to *The Godbearing Life*

YOUTH AND RELATIONSHIPS

Coupled with assurance and affirmation, teens need relationships. In addition to being accepted by peers, they also desire adult models. But relationships with adults can be problematic. As teens break away from authority, they're threatened by some adult relationships—including those with parents, law enforcement officials, employers, church hierarchy, and school officials. Rather than being subservient to adults, teens would rather form friendships—a feeling of mutual respect with an opportunity to look up to adults and to see them as role models.

Beth Slevcove, spiritual director and staff member of Youth Specialties, believes that sometimes just an adult presence is enough. "My presence is permission giving. I can say to kids that it's okay to pay attention to your journey with God. Paying attention is really worth doing. It is important for teens to have an adult take time to hold a young person in a compassionate space." A key to working with teenagers in a spiritual setting is just that—being in a compassionate space, or just hanging out. Rarely does a high school student request classical one-on-one spiritual direction. Most of the time, the spiritual companionship happens "on the fly" or in a situation in which the teen and the adult are just hanging out. A youth pastor told a story to a group of us who were attending a conference on parenting adolescents in Minneapolis about the father who took his teenage son to lunch at McDonalds—in Duluth, a three-hour drive. This father and his son probably passed a dozen McDonalds restaurants on their way to Duluth, but the six-hour round-trip journey placed each in the other's presence with nothing else to do but talk.

That safe adult presence is especially appealing to youth in inner-city churches. From my interviews with youth workers in these churches, I learned that providing a safe place is the key to doing youth ministry in the city and in the first-ring suburbs. The church building must be safe, and the adults who work with the youth must be accepting and nonjudgmental. The building and the people represent a place that's vastly different from the chaos of the young people's lives. Youth pastors in inner-city situations have told me that kids come to youth group for the peace. They enjoy the simple and quiet prayer and conversations where they can share their stories in safety and form relationships with people who care about them.

Associate minister and youth worker Lorinda Clausson of Presbyterian Church of the Master in Minneapolis sums up the needs of high school youth: "It's all about relationships. Sometimes," she says, "a teen is comfortable initiating a relationship," and she shared a story to illustrate her point. A high school student began to ask her questions about his faith, and she responded by reaching out and connecting with him. They went out for coffee a few times and talked about God and about Christian beliefs. After some time, he brought a friend along who had similar questions. Soon five more joined, and she and the group began to meet at a coffee shop once a week. They called themselves the Nerd Squad. After the group grew to twenty, they needed to meet at the church because the coffee shop was too small. When I asked Lorinda why these teens wanted to meet, she replied, "I think they wanted someone to listen to them. They want an adult who has struggled with faith questions and who is not shocked by their questions."

> "Society frequently devalues teenagers, sometimes even viewing them as obstacles to adult freedom and happiness. Teens are often viewed as less than—less intelligent, less spiritual, less prudent, less wise. . . . How far from the truth. On the contrary, teens are an untapped resource of great spirituality, strength, sensibility and wisdom."
>
> –Peter Tassi, *Beauty Within: Inspirational Stories and Practical Advice for Anyone Who Works (or Lives) with Teenagers,* ix.

NATIONAL STUDY OF YOUTH AND RELIGION

This story illustrates the interest today's teens have in faith issues. The National Study of Youth and Religion in the United States, the most comprehensive survey ever done on faith and adolescents, found that more than 80 percent of youth say religion is important in their lives. Teens who attend weekly services and belong to a youth group are less likely to use alcohol and drugs, are less likely to have premarital sex. They feel better about themselves, do better in school, and make moral choices based on what's right rather than on what's "in." A belief in God can give teens the ability to resist the pervasive temptations of today's culture, and adult companions can affirm youths' ability to make wise choices. (www.youthandreligion.org)

WHAT IS NEEDED TO WORK WITH YOUTH?

For those called to companion high school students—whether they're youth pastors or moms who ride on the band bus—much is required. The adult needs to be genuine and to be willing to learn from the young person. The adult needs to listen and to affirm the youth's questions and concerns. Adolescence is a time when a young person's self concept takes a dive. An adult can help a youth reclaim and affirm the youth's self-confidence. Adolescence is also a time for experimentation with sex, drugs, reckless driving, unsupervised parties, gangs, and extreme sports. An adult companion must be willing to confront the teen with his or her experimentation and to present the ramifications of risky behavior.

BEING A COMPANION TO STUDENTS IN POSTSECONDARY SCHOOLS

Anyone enrolled in a postsecondary school—from a vocational school to a four-year college, from seminary to graduate school—is under tremendous stress. Typical stressors include achievement or grade-point average, the challenges of being away from home for the first time, the pressures surrounding campus social life, financial worries, the anxiety of managing a job, social life (or possibly marriage), and school, the uncertainty of life after graduation, and the confusion associated with rethinking previous moral and theological paradigms.

In addition, those in postsecondary schools are no longer adolescents. They're young adults, and they're busy being young adults. In *Big Questions, Worthy Dreams*, Sharon Daloz Parks says it well:

> *They seek work, find work, change their work. They party and play. They earn undergraduate, master's, doctoral and professional degrees. They have a yen for travel—from one country to another, and from one company to another. Sometimes they protest and make demands, for themselves, and on behalf of others. They create art, claim adventure, explore and establish long-term relationships, form house-holds, volunteer in their communities, become parents, initiate important projects, and serve internships. They try to become financially independent. They also go to prison. Some*

deal with major health and other physical and emotional changes. And some young adults die too young.[2]

Having an adult companion during their college or vocational school years can prove invaluable to students. They have opportunities to use the services of a college counselor or a professor. Those in Christian schools can seek counsel from a campus minister, a chaplain, a spiritual director, or a person associated with their church. Spiritual director Kim Jacobson works with high school youth in her church in Fargo, North Dakota. When they graduate, she continues to correspond with them while they are in college, and she meets with them during vacations. "They say it means a lot to them that I send them handwritten letters asking how school is going and how they are connecting with God," she says. "It is time-consuming to hand write, but it is the key to staying connected, and the rewards outweigh the hand cramps."

AREAS OF CONCERN

In my interviews with those who work with college-age students as advisors or companions, most stated that there are several areas of major concern for this population: time pressures, relationships, lifestyle choices, vocational decisions, and faith questions.

The number-one stressor of the postsecondary students I interviewed is time pressure. One student said, "There is so much to do, work, classes, studying, research, dating, and not enough time." A question advisors and spiritual directors often ask of students is: What can you do to lighten your load? "College students are often pressured beyond their capacity," says a spiritual director who meets with a group of five students twice a month. "As their spiritual companion, I listen to their stories of heavy workloads and frustration, and I help them organize their time and their responsibilities. I also suggest ways to balance work, study, social activities, rest, and connection with God. This is especially helpful to freshmen and sophomores who arrive on campus without a clue, and who often panic when the work load becomes too heavy."

Another stressor includes the many opportunities, both healthy and potentially unhealthy, that are presented to students. Young people have the freedom to explore academic opportunities such as study abroad and internships, but they also have opportunities to test the waters of potentially dangerous situations such as drinking, drugs, gambling, and extreme sports. Those who work with college-age students have observed that a major question in the minds of many of these students is: What's okay for me to try? An objective adult companion can listen and allow a student to explore his options and to teach him some discernment tools.

Teaching discernment tools allows students to enter into a deeper connection with God.

A recent study has indicated that connection with God is a high priority for many college students. The University of California at Los Angeles conducted a multiyear Spirituality in Higher Education project to determine spiritual trends and patterns among college students. The pilot survey was conducted in the year 2000 with 3,680 freshmen attending forty-six diverse colleges and universities across the United States (private secular, private religious, and public). Each student completed a follow-up questionnaire in the spring of 2003. The summary of their findings included:

There is a high level of spiritual engagement and commitment among college students, with more than half placing a high value on integrating spirituality in their lives (58%), 77% saying "we are all spiritual beings," and 71% indicating they "gain spiritual strength by trusting in a higher power." Substantial numbers of students, upwards of 84%, have had a spiritual experience at least occasionally (e.g., witnessing the beauty and harmony of nature, listening to beautiful music). Regarding perspectives on religion, among the third-year college students surveyed, three in four report that they pray, that religion is personally helpful to them, and that they discuss religion and spirituality with friends."[3]

Inviting a student to stay close to God is what a spiritual companion can do. Much of what I said in chapters two and three can be applied to this college-age population—especially the ideas surrounding the topics of discernment and vocation—but I want to stress the importance of companionship with these people. They need someone willing to listen to them and to gently guide them. One young man at a Christian college told me that going to chapel a couple times a week helps, but it's not enough to keep him connected to God. When I asked what more he needs, he replied, "It would help me to talk to someone—someone older, someone who would really care about me."

I'm not sure it's important to have a highly structured spiritual program for college-age people. They already live in a structured setting. Episcopal youth minister, Lisa Kimball, of Minneapolis says that what works with college-age people is space and rhythm—having a definite time to meet and then space, both physical and psychological space, to talk about faith issues.

SEMINARY STUDENTS AND SPIRITUAL DIRECTION

Jane Vennard, spiritual director and adjunct faculty member of the Iliff School of theology in Denver, Colorado, says:

> *More and more students in Protestant seminaries are seeking spiritual directors. These students recognize their need to inte-grate their academic studies with their spiritual journeys and realize that without intentional spiritual practices they could forget the call from God that brought them to seminary in the first place. They long to discover their wholeness so that they can serve God and others from the depths of who they are and who they are becoming."*[4]

SPECIAL NEEDS OF SEMINARY STUDENTS

Everything we've explored about college-age students applies to seminary students as well. But seminarians have an extra load to carry as they prepare to be in Christian ministry. Since ministry is to be their occupation, it's essential that they have a spiritual director or participate in group spiritual direction for their self-care and for their spiritual growth. Jason, a youth pastor, remarked, "In seminary, I learned how to work myself to death. There were no opportunities to learn habits of self-care. I would highly encourage seminarians to develop self care habits now before they graduate because once you get into ministry, the work overwhelms you." Dawn, another seminary graduate, added, "In seminary we learn to question our faith. We deconstruct faith, but we also need to reconstruct that faith. That's where spiritual direction can help."

Jane Vennard talks about the issues seminary students bring into spiritual direction: issues of discernment regarding their future in the church; issues of self-care such as use of time and prioritizing their lives; theological issues such as the balance between the academic (the mind) and the spiritual (the heart). In my own work with seminary students and recent graduates of seminary programs who are in our spiritual direction preparation program, I've noticed that, generally speaking, seminaries are primarily academic institutions. Of course they need to be, but are they fully preparing students for ministry in the real world? Is there a balance between the academic and the practical? Are seminary students taught to care for their own spiritual lives? Do seminary students grow in love for God and in relationship with Christ while in seminary? Do these future church leaders learn to pray—not just say prayers—in seminary? Do they nurture a rich inner life where the Holy Spirit dwells and where their strength for ministry is located?

The Reverend Dr. A. J. van den Blink of the department of pastoral theology at Colgate Rochester Divinity School in Rochester, New York, provides insight to these questions: "My experience with theological education, both as a student in the 1960s and later as a faculty member at two seminaries, is that there is more talk about God than reflection on experiences of God."[5] Van den Blink explains that, beginning with the Age of Enlightenment and the scientific discoveries of the 1800s, seminaries moved away from being centers of spiritual formation to being centers of academia. Van den Blink continues, "Spiritual formation came to be seen as incidental to the real work of theological education, namely that of intellectual formation. The result has been a widening gap between theology and the practice of ministry, between prayer and action, between seminary and parish, and also between academic and spiritual formation."[6] One seminary student I interviewed spoke with passion as he summarized van den Blink's ideas: "Words and ideas are not enough. I need relationships, and I need God."[7]

Seminary students need relationships as well as a safe place to focus on how God is present in their lives. Jane Vennard quotes a student who wrote about his spiritual-direction relationship, "In an environment that pulls me every which way, spiritual direction has helped me stay grounded in God."[8] A spiritual director/mentor/companion can listen to the frustrations and the questions of seminary students, encourage them in prayer and silence, and help them with discernment towards ministry. This seminary student continues, "I don't think I would be here if I had not had the opportunity to sort and sift through all my conflicting feelings about being called to the ministry."[9]

I had the privilege of supervising a master of divinity student as an intern for a year. Every Monday morning Lori and I took an extended time to pray together. She would lead the prayer one week, I the next. Those times of prayer were invaluable to each of us. It allowed us to begin the week recognizing just why we are in Christian ministry. Those prayer times set a tone for the week, enabling us to spend time in silence, listening to the voice that would guide us during the week. In Lori's final evaluation of the year, she cited those Monday prayer times as one of the most valuable experiences of her internship.

Being in Christian ministry in any capacity is challenging and exhausting. It's easy to lose ourselves in the lives of others and in the administrative tasks, and it's even easier to forget our own self-care and to ignore our spiritual hunger. A spiritual companion can remind us to pay attention to our longings and to our questions. A spiritual mentor can remind us to notice God in all of the activities of life and to rely on the guidance of the Spirit. Those in seminary must be prepared for the work of ministry by being enabled to practice the art of listening to God.

BEING A COMPANION TO OLDER ADULTS WHOSE LIVES ARE IMPACTED BY YOUTH

It's not uncommon to provide spiritual direction to the parent or a grandparent of a young person, or to someone challenged by the postmodern church. As a spiritual director, I hear concerns such as:

- My teenage son refuses to go to church, and it is creating family tension.
- I am ready to leave our church. It no longer attends to my hunger for spiritual growth. But the rest of my family wants to stay.
- I raised my daughter in a good Christian home. Now I see her drifting away from Christian morals.
- My son is not raising his children in a church community. Should I say something?
- My daughter is participating in meditation practices. I'm not sure that is even Christian.
- We have a new pastor who is leading us in lectio divina, and I don't know what to think.

It is an understatement to say that Western culture has changed at an alarming rate in the last decades, more than at any other time in history. Furthermore, all aspects of life have changed—entertainment, the work environment, education, politics, science, technology, medicine, and religion. Many people are frustrated and confused by the changes they see in church doctrine, theology, church administration, and pastoral care. Moreover, many older adults see young people practice Christianity in ways that seem foreign.

As spiritual companions, we can journey with these people by gently allowing them to express their fear, confusion, and concern. We can be aware of generational differences and the historical context in which older adults were raised. We can listen to the angst in their hearts, and we can bring them to God. I like to use reflections questions with these directees.

- Where is God present in this situation with your daughter?
- What is the flavor of the conversations you and your son are having?
- What are you hearing as you take this to prayer?
- Say more about the fear/confusion/hurt you feel.
- Can you talk about the frustration you are experiencing at your church?

- What is different in Christianity today from several decades ago?
- If you were a young person today, how would you practice your Christian faith?

Finally, as companions to older adults who are affected by the religious changes of today, we might need to say a few things about today's Christian climate and point directees to reference material.

WRAP-UP

I began this chapter by referring to *The Godbearing Life*. The word *Godbearing* is a good one. It describes what older adults can do for young people. Adult mentors can accompany young people through decisions, crises, and questions. Companions can also serve as role models— models of people who have experienced similar life situations and who have survived. Daren, 23, says it well: "When I am with my mentor, I have hope. I know I can survive this crisis, because I know Dave is here for me, and I know God is here. I'm not alone."

NOTES

1. Kenda Creasy Dean and Ron Foster, *The Godbearing Life* (Nashville: Upper Room Books, 1998), 16.

2. Sharon Daloz Parks, *Big Questions, Worthy Dreams: Mentoring Young Adults in Their Search for Meaning, Purpose, and Faith* (San Francisco: Jossey-Bass, 2000), 5.

3. See http://spirituality.ucla.edu/about spirituality.

4. Jane Vennard, "Spiritual Direction with Seminary Students," *Presence: The Journal of Spiritual Directors International* (October 2003): 9.

5. Rose Mary Dougherty, "Group Spiritual Direction in Seminary," *The Lived Experience of Group Spiritual Direction* (Mahwah, NJ: Paulist Press, 2003), 214.

6. Ibid., 215.

7. Vennard, "Spiritual Direction with Seminary Students," 11.

8. Ibid.

9. Ibid.

CHAPTER SIX

PREPARING HOLY COMPANIONS

Being a spiritual companion to a young person is vital work in today's Christian environment. Spiritual mentors are preparing leadership for tomorrow's church, which will continue to be actively engaged in the world, with all its issues and debates. Tomorrow's leaders will also inherit the social and religious issues of today, including debates surrounding popular culture and the church, medical ethics, armed conflict, poverty, civil rights, and terrorism. And who could possibly know what other issues will emerge as the years progress?

Those who companion tomorrow's leaders will need to be prepared to be open, accepting, and non-judgmental. Not everyone is called to this ministry; but those who feel an inclination in this direction need to know that much is required. There are five essential qualities necessary for those who work with youth and young adults: a sense of call, a life of prayer, an authentic spirit, knowledge of self, and a sense of humor.

A SENSE OF CALL

The first step in enabling adults to work with young people is for the older adult to have a sense of call from God for this ministry. This is a discernment process that involves prayer, questioning, and discussion with others. Good questions to ask in this discernment process include:

- What is inside of me that is motivating me to desire to work with young people?
- As I take this decision to prayer, what am I hearing?
- What are others saying to me?
- What gifts do I have that would make me a good listener to young people?

Engaging in a discernment process enables a person to come before God and others with honesty and humility. Moreover, the discernment process is, in itself, good preparation for working with youth and young adults.

The chronological age of a youth worker is of little importance. In my interviews with young adults, the question I frequently asked was: Does age matter in people who accompany you? The answer I received 100 percent of the time was "no." Young adults are looking for authenticity and acceptance. I believe the Holy Spirit pays little attention to age. Youth worker Faye was surprised when she was asked to work with young people. "I never considered working with this age group," she said. "Teens are scary, and I tend to shy away from them. Besides, I am so much older than they. I have gray hair, for heaven's sake." Yet, as Faye pondered this invitation and as she spent time in prayer, she felt her heart begin to reach out to the adolescents and young adults in her congregation. She started to see youth in a different light. "They began to worm their way into my heart."

A Life of Prayer

During my interview process, I spent time with two youth ministers on staff in a large congregation. One was 24, the other, 31. In the course of our conversation, I asked, "What's most hard for you in ministry?" I expected answers such as budget concerns, fatigue, and inability to spend time with youth because of administrative tasks; but their identical answers surprised me. Both agreed that they struggle most with being a model of what they teach. They struggle with being a Christian in today's world, and they struggle with prayer. Both emphasized prayer in their ministry with youth, and both realized that they must be praying persons if they are to model that kind of life with their young people.

The adage of practicing what you preach is essential in working with today's teens and twentysomethings. It fuels an authentic life, and it leads to a life of prayer. Working with young people isn't easy. While they're delightful and often wise beyond their years, they're also unpredictable and emotional. Sometimes their lives are impacted by tragedy. Youth workers need to stay close to God in their ministry and care for their own spiritual needs.

An Authentic Spirit

Older adults don't need to assume the aura of popular culture in order to work with the younger generations. They don't need to know what music is "in." It's not a requirement to know about the latest fashions, or video games, or film. What matters is authenticity. Youth relate to people who genuinely care for them and who are real. Moreover, young people like to know about us; they like to hear our stories. They want to know about our struggles and how we coped. They want to hear the faith questions we've asked—and the ones we're still asking. Transitioning into adulthood is scary, and young people need to look at us and see how we made the transition. Adults working with youth need to be able to share their stories, with honesty, when appropriate.

Self-Knowledge

To achieve the authenticity that youth admire, adults must have a strong sense of self. It's important for adults to have done some self-exploration into areas of personality, gifts, passions, temptations, and weaknesses, and to have a sense of how their adolescent and young adult years differ from today's culture. It's helped me, for example, to be aware of the social, religious, and historical context of my young adult life and how those contexts have shaped me, and to know what I value today and what I've tossed out over the decades. And it's important to know how the era of my own teen and young adult years differs from today's culture. I believe that personal reflection and self-exploration lead to self-awareness and authenticity, which, in turn, inspire the confidence of young people.

A SENSE OF HUMOR

A mantra I often recite is: We Christians take ourselves too seriously. Fortunately, youth remind us to lighten up, to take time to play and explore and allow our creativity to flourish. They help us remember our youth—to value it and to listen to its lessons. A sense of humor helps us cope with the maturing process of youth, especially adolescence, and to remember that the young people we companion are not finished with their growing. Scientists who have conducted recent studies of the adolescent brain speculate that the frontal lobe, responsible for impulse control, is still being developed. (Anyone who has raised a teenager doesn't need a study to prove that!) A sense of humor is valuable as we realize that sometimes youth can't help being impulsive and random. Sometimes we just need to sit back and enjoy young people and laugh with them. Spiritual director Sandra Gray offers this advice: "Let young people be who they are, then help them identify with the gifts they have. Give them opportunities to use those strengths, and help them notice God in their lives."

Coupled with a sense of humor is the need to hold agendas lightly. Older adults need to be as agenda free as possible when working with youth. Their interest and energy shift minute by minute. When working with young people, flexibility and the ability to laugh make the ministry easier and more effective.

THE PREPARATION PROCESS

I don't have a magic formula called "How to Train Spiritual Mentors." I've learned that when one works with matters of faith, rigid formulas stifle the Spirit of God. Those who prepare people for ministry need to be aware of their own unique circumstances. They need to listen to God's guidance and to pay attention to others, including those whom they serve. Enabling people to be spiritual companions is not taught like computer programming or geology. Potential spiritual mentors arrive with an abundance of experiences and gifts that beg to be resurrected and studied. This study can be achieved through reflection on the following:.

Reflection on the Faith of Today's Youth

One of the greatest surprises I encountered as I conducted my interviews is that young people—the churched and the unchurched—know more about faith than I had imagined. Adults who companion youth and young adults must realize that young people aren't blank slates waiting for someone to write the answers on their hearts or to tell them what to believe. "Teens are not empty vessels," says Sandra Gray, "nor does what's in the vessel need to be changed." There's something—lots of some-things—in the hearts and minds of today's younger generations. They have stories, experiences, questions, and ideas. Our role as companions is to listen with respect, without an agenda, and without a desire to change them. We need to listen to their stories, to ponder them, and, through a prayerful reflection, to allow God to teach us how to minister to these young people.

Reflection on the Shift in Worldview

As an early baby boomer, my adolescent and young adult years were the decades of the sixties and seventies. The young people I work with today grew up in later decades. The difference in the religious culture of those decades is astounding. Religion today, especially in the United States, is out of the closet and even sometimes "in your face." This paradigm was far from true when I was a teen and young adult. During those years, one's faith was either a very private affair, or it was thought to be not as relevant as science. Authors Strauss and Howe describe this era and how it differs from the current one:

> *Boomers grew up back in a highly secular era, when newsweek-lies asked if God was dead, when politicians almost never mentioned religion, and when adults helped kids seek scientific answers to religious questions. The premise was that this would help kids think more for themselves. Religion was not something most kids could comfortably display at a public school. By contrast, Millennials are growing up in a spiritually driven era, when newsweeklies announce that God is back, when politicians chatter incessantly about faith, and when adults help kids seek faith-based answers to secular questions.*[1]

Perhaps the shift in today's religious climate is one reason for this book. I want people in my own generation to understand something of today's Christian world, of the way contemporary society views religion, and of the young who are being formed in their faith under the influence of today's paradigms.

I encourage those who prepare adults for youth and young adult ministry to spend time in a discussion of these societal changes. I believe that lack of understanding of today's mainstreaming of Christianity could be a hindrance to working with younger generations. Ponder these questions: What religious messages are today's young people receiving? Where are they getting these messages? How do they decide which to believe and which to ignore? How can we help them discern? What about our own beliefs? What belief system did we come from? What do we believe now? How did we get here? What have we thrown out and what do we still believe? What still puzzles us? What process did we use to shape our current religious thought and belief? And a final question, based on the above reflection: How are we to be with our young people?

REFLECTION ON THE MINISTRY OF SPIRITUAL MENTORSHIP

I would begin this study by having the adults spend considerable time reflecting on the mentors in their own lives. Some possible questions:

- Who were those mentors/companions?
- What drew you to them?
- What did you learn from them?
- What qualities would you like to mimic as you work with young people?
- What qualities would you choose not to use with youth?

These questions can be processed and discussed with the other adults on the ministry team; then applied to your own situation.

REFLECTION ON THE GOSPELS

An important component in preparing adults for youth ministry is to invite them to immerse themselves in the gospels. The person of Jesus and the indwelling of his Spirit are what will enable people to be holy companions. If I were preparing a group of adults for ministry to young people, I would encourage them to spend extended time slowly reading the gospels, and I would join in that process. I would invite them to be present in the story, using all their senses, to observe how Jesus responds to people. For example, through reading the story of Jesus teaching the multitudes, I'd bring my adult leaders to the edge of a crowd and observe how Jesus takes pity on the people, notices their hunger, and feeds them. Or in another story, I'd encourage my adults to awaken with Jesus long before dawn, and I would invite them to follow Jesus to a lonely place to pray. How is Jesus praying? What is he saying? Can you join him in prayer? And one of my favorites, I'd invite all of us to be in the crowd as Jesus summons Zacchaeus from the tree. How does the crowd react to Zacchaeus? How do we feel about Jesus' choice? What's it like to be going with Jesus to Zaccheus's house? What do we learn about ourselves as we enter into this story? What do we learn about how to minister to young people?

Through this reflective reading of the gospels, I'd encourage my adult leaders to watch Jesus as he listens, touches, heals—as he weeps, tells stories, curses, laughs, and dances. Finally, I'd ask my adult leaders to frequently reflect on the words from the concluding chapters of John's gospel: "I do not call you servants any longer, because the servant does not know what the master is doing, but I have called you friends, because I have made known to you everything that I have heard from my Father. You did not choose me but I chose you. And I appointed you to go and bear fruit, fruit that will last, so that the Father will give you whatever you ask him in my name. I am giving you these commands so that you may love one another" (John 14:15–17).

Our greatest spiritual mentor is Jesus—the way he lived his life, the way he touched the hearts of people, and the way he confronted with truth. Through reflective immersion into Jesus' life, we learn how to be better people and how to work with our young.

PREPARING COMPANIONS IN A COMMUNAL SETTING

While potential youth and young adult workers can spend personal time reflecting on the ways of Jesus, I believe adults can best be prepared to companion young people by coming together in a communal setting and sharing those ponderings. A group setting provides a number of benefits.

Accountability and ongoing support. In this setting, the group can learn from each other and have accountability and ongoing support. Associate minister Lorinda Clausson, of Presbyterian Church of the Master in Minneapolis, intentionally forms community with her adult leaders. "I have a core group of ten leaders, and we meet once a week," she explains. "Our first priority is to pray for the kids, and we take this seriously. But we also have fun; we share of our lives. It's awesome for me to see the trust we have of one another. We share a common love of adolescents, and we have a sense of humor." In addition to building community with her adult leaders, Lorinda believes that the leaders model Christian community for her youth. "I believe that the way the leaders are together, the kids will be."

Opportunities for prayer and planning. Youth minister Steve Matthews draws his adult leaders together twice a month for prayer and planning. They begin their time together with a period of silence followed by a check-in that allows people to share—not "fix." Group members are asked to be holy listeners. The group then participates in a session of *lectio divina*. As they reflect on a scripture passage, they ask the question: Is there a word here for us and for this ministry? Sometimes the group does an Ignatian examen, in which the participants reflect on the previous youth group meeting and ask questions such as: When were we most open to God during that meeting? When did we seem blocked? Where was God that evening? Once the group has taken the time for prayer and reflection, the planning portion is easy, because the spiritual needs of the group members are met and they are free to be attentive to the Spirit. Steve firmly believes that adults must be grounded in their own faith and must be willing to be stretched in their faith before they can minister to youth.

A communal setting allows participants to attend to their own faith journey and to seek the guidance of the Holy Spirit. It also allows group members to hold each another accountable for self-care by encouraging each other to take time for prayer and to balance work, rest, and recreation.

A setting to address problems. Other accountability issues can be addressed in a communal setting, and questions and concerns can be

brought before the group. When working with young people, special
boundaries need to be observed. Adult mentors can easily slip into the
role of substitute parent or glorified hero. There *are* times when a
spiritual companion does take on some parental characteristics, such as
listening, affirming, and caring. But those characteristics are within the
context of his or her role as group leader, spiritual director, or youth pastor. A youth pastor or spiritual companion is not the young person's
parent. He or she hasn't raised this person from infancy nor been responsible in the same way a parent is. This frees the spiritual director or youth
pastor to be a more objective, affirming presence. It's sometimes difficult
for the family of a teen or young adult to be objective. Young people live
with their families—who see them at their worst—and they often have a
history of struggle. Young people are fortunate if they have several adults
in their lives in addition to their parents, but it is important to mention
that each of the adults fulfills a different role.

The transition into adulthood is confusing and frightening. Young
people need to observe the behavior of healthy adults, but sometimes
this can lead to a kind of hero-worship. Healthy adults need to be aware
of this, as well as of their own desire to be loved and appreciated. Several
unhealthy tendencies can emerge when working with youth, and it's possible for adults to satisfy their need for love or self-esteem through their
youth work. For example, adult companions can see qualities in a young
person they don't see in their own children, and this can lead to envy.
Adults can become jealous of the opportunities today's young people
have at their disposal. These unhealthy tendencies need to be honestly
confronted before God in prayer and sometimes before the community
of other adult youth leaders. A community of fellow youth workers can
watch one another for unhealthy tendencies. I mentioned in chapter
three my tendency to want to parent young people when I began to see
them in spiritual direction. My peer supervision group was quick to alert
me to that tendency.

A process for honest evaluation. Finally, preparing adults in a communal setting allows for honest evaluation. Youth pastors can gather
their adult volunteers regularly to reflect on the direction of the
ministry. What is being communicated to our youth? How is it being
communicated? What are we not communicating? What do we sense

we need to incorporate into our youth meetings? What are the kids saying they need? Asking the young people is an essential part of the evaluation process with questions such as: What has worked for you these past months at youth group? What hasn't worked? Where have you noticed God's presence? Doing this evaluative process in a discerning manner allows the Holy Spirit to have the freedom to guide the discussion. This discernment process includes opening with a time of prayer that will lead to some silence, then allowing for a pause during the discussion for times of quiet prayer—especially when the group seems stuck. Moments of "stuckness" often allow for a freshness of the Spirit to enter into the discussion.

PREPARING SPIRITUAL DIRECTORS FOR A CHURCH IN TRANSITION: THE CHRISTOS CENTER MODEL

As each year of this new millennium passes, a greater diversity of people come to Christos to receive spiritual direction or to be prepared as spiritual directors. This diversity includes people with a wide range of denominational backgrounds, as well as people of differing ages. In recent years, more young adults have come to Christos Center to receive spiritual direction and to be prepared as spiritual directors. This is a growing trend, and I've had to make adjustments for this new population of seekers. I carefully pair young people seeking spiritual direction with spiritual directors who I know are comfortable working with young adults. I interview those applying to our spiritual direction preparation program, Tending the Holy: Preparation for the Ministry of Spiritual Direction, just as I would interview older adults.

There is no minimum age requirement for the Tending the Holy program. When I was hired by Christos Center to coordinate the program in 1997, all applicants had to be at least 35 years old. One of the first policies I implemented was to open the program to adults of all ages. Slowly the age demographic changed, and there was a wider range of applicants. The graduating class of 2001 was the first to demonstrate that demographic change. The youngest member was 29, the oldest, 71. By journeying together for two years, the people in that class gained respect for each end of the age spectrum. I've found that one's chronological age doesn't necessarily determine the spiritual and personal maturity needed to enter a spiritual direction preparation program. What does matter are life experiences, personal spiritual growth, and a call from God.

The ministry of spiritual direction today is a growing and expanding ministry reaching out across faith traditions, and those who graduate from our program are called to minister in a myriad of ways: classical one-on-one spiritual director, group spiritual director, spiritual director to people on the margins of society, spiritual director within the context of a youth group, spiritual companion to the elderly, retreat leader, faith-sharing group leader, workshop leader, prayer ministry team member, missionary, prayer garden host, twelve-step facilitator, Befriender/Stephen minister, worship leader, pilgrimage leader, mission trip mentor, church planter, writer, and artist. Moreover, some of our graduates have brought spiritual direction principles into their secular workplace. Others have brought spiritual-direction tools into their helping professions of pastor, youth pastor/worker, parish nurse, psychologist, social worker, physical therapist, occupational therapist, and massage therapist,

As spiritual direction expands into a variety of ministry settings and attracts a wider diversity of applicants, our program at Christos cannot remain stagnant. Each summer I gather with the group facilitators, the people who directly nurture each participant, and we prayerfully discern the changes we are to make in the program. In recent years, our changes have fallen into two general categories: technique and content.

TECHNIQUE
Christos Center has been preparing spiritual directors since 1990, and the teaching style has been within the context of community. Presenters (faculty and group facilitators) and participants are in relationship, and we intentionally form a learning community. This style reflects a simple paradigm that Parker Palmer suggests in *To Know as We Are Known: Education as a Spiritual Journey.* "Learning does not happen," he writes, "until students are brought into relationship with the teacher, with each other, and with the subject."[2]

The predominant method of delivery for our program has been lecture, but in recent years, our style has shifted to a more contemplative and experiential one. The real teacher is the Spirit of God, so presenters are asked to pause halfway through their talks and call for moments of silence while all reflect on the suggestions and concepts. Participants are sometimes asked to pause and journal on a portion of the presentation and then report in a group setting. Assigned papers aren't reports but are prayerful reflections. Participants are asked to prepare a monthly reflection paper that invites them to notice where God was present during the month and to notice how the class work has affected their personal spiritual growth. During Advent, class members are invited to take a day of silent retreat and process that day in their reflection papers. During Lent, class members are encouraged to create a spiritual practice for themselves.

Once a year, the monthly reflection is a project or an experience. One project we've used is called "A Meditation on People," created by spiritual director Kathy Huber. Participants are encouraged to place themselves for at least two hours in a setting outside their comfort zone, such as a bus station, an ethnic restaurant, a food pantry, a coffee house, an upscale shopping mall, a thrift store, or a church service very different from their own. Class participants are instructed to notice those around them and to reflect on questions such as: As you begin to observe a person, what is your first impression? As time passes, how does that impression change? Imagine what gives that person joy? Pain? Imagine what the person may want for his or her children? For him- or herself? How are you like this person? Where do you see Christ in this person? Finally, class members are to spend some time praying in silence for the person they have been observing. People who participate in our program feel this exercise has led to profound insights.

New to our program this year is an experience I call "The Emerging Church." The second-year class is invited to explore suggested Web pages, interview young people or older people about their faith, or attend a church service or para-church activity that's called either postmodern, contemporary, or emergent. Or they're invited to visit a faith-based organization doing social action work. As class participants make their visits, they're asked to reflect on what they're seeing and place their observations in the context of spiritual direction. The purpose of this project is to increase awareness of how the church is changing and how the ministry of spiritual direction can act as a catalyst.

Members from other parts of the United States and from foreign countries join the Christos learning community in Minnesota. Each "home" class in St. Paul, Minnesota, has a cohort of distance learners who, through technology, are members of our learning community. People come from places such as Madison, Wisconsin; Grand Forks, North Dakota; Siloam Springs, Arkansas; Grand Junction, Colorado; Fargo, North Dakota; Marshall, Michigan; Orange City, Iowa; Pune, India; Copenhagen, Denmark; France, Singapore, and Japan. There were so many people in the Chicago, Illinois, area taking our distance-learning program that we started a satellite program in 2003 in the western Chicago suburbs.

Personal transformation is a vital part of the spiritual direction preparation program. At Christos, we expect our participants to continue to be transformed into the image of Christ through their own prayers, their church communities, and the content of the preparation program. Prayer is always a central focus of each of our classes. Class begins with a twenty-minute prayer experience that incorporates time for silence. Class participants in the second year of the program lead the twenty-minute opening prayer experience and often rely on the classical prayer forms of *lectio divina*, centering prayer, Christian meditation, body movement, images, music, ritual, and art forms.

These components of communal and experiential learning, personal transformation, and contemplative prayer reflect the style of the Tending the Holy program—a style that enables people to minister to the church as it shifts into a new era.

CONTENT

Christos Center is fortunate to attract not only a diverse age range, but members of a diverse range of denominations as well. As the age and denominational backgrounds of our participants have broadened, so has the content of our program. In the second year of our program, we include presentations on how life experiences and life state affect one's spirituality. We study young adult stages, midlife, aging, gender differences, personality, and differences in denominational background—all within the context of the spiritual direction relationship. A Saturday morning class is devoted to the other ministries to which a spiritual director can be called: group spiritual direction, retreat ministry, faith-sharing groups, and educational forums. In addition, our class participants have an option to serve as intern spiritual companions through an organization in Minneapolis called City House, which provides spiritual companionship to people who are not usually thought of as candidates for spiritual direction: the homeless, people in halfway houses, people in prisons, and those in drug rehabilitation centers.

Several times a year, workshops are offered to our alumni and current participants on topics such as male spirituality, spiritual formation for churches, spiritual direction for young adults, and spiritual direction with people in addiction recovery or affected by someone in recovery.

This attention to variety in our spiritual direction preparation program allows spiritual companionship to be more than just the classical paradigm of two middle-aged people sitting across from each other with a candle in the middle, and places it into a postmodern society of unsurpassed diversity.

WRAP-UP

Today's youth culture, hungry for spiritual food, is reclaiming spiritual companionship. The demographic of those seeking this companionship is no longer bound to the categories of white, female, middle-aged, and middle class. As the director of a center that prepares people for the ministry of spiritual direction, I must pay attention to the new groups seeking companionship.

A FINAL WORD: HUNGRY SOULS AND HOLY COMPANIONS IN AN ANCIENT-FUTURE CHRISTIAN CULTURE

Through four years of interviews and conversations with youth, young adults, and those who companion them, and through the spiritual discipline of writing this book, I've come to realize that in many respects today's youthful seekers are not that different from past generations. They have the same passions, drives, and questions. What's different, however, is the culture of today's Western society.

As Western society has evolved, its evolutionary process has gone through numerous shifts: from an industry-driven society to an information age; from dweller spirituality to seeker spirituality; from a God held under "wraps" to an explosive God present in every aspect of life; and from a concept of a controlling God to a personal God who invites creation into freedom. Christian society today is working out the ramifications of that freedom by engaging in conversation among denominations, faith traditions, gender, race, and age. It's a freedom that understands that no one faith or no single generation has all the truth. We need each other. We need the experience and stability of older adults and we need the freshness and daring of youth.

Today's Western culture, with its modern conveniences and hyperactive lifestyle, finds itself looking to the past to find spiritual truth. This strange oxymoron of ancient/future describes where we are today. It's a good place to be, because it combines the wisdom of the ages with the possibilities of the future. It's an era where today's young people can become lost if they do not have "Godbearers"—holy people who can listen and can point young people to Jesus, to a Companion who says, "Know that I am with you always, even to the end of the age."

NOTES

1. William Strauss and Neil Howe, *New Millennials Rising: The Next Great Generation* (New York: Vintage Books, 2000), 235.

2. Parker Palmer, *To Know as We Are Known: Education as a Spiritual Journey* (New York: HarperSanFrancisco, 1993), xvi.

BIBLIOGRAPHY

HIGHLY RECOMMENDED RESOURCES

WEB PAGES

Explore Faith, www.explorefaith.org. Up-to-date world news as well as
current information on popular culture. Includes devotional material,
the Daily Office, and commentaries on film, books, and music.
Commentaries include questions to ask to facilitate discussion on
current film and books.

Method X (The Way of Christ), www.methodx.net. An online Christian
community where young adults can identify and explore their
relationship with God and others. Excellent source of global news for
young people. Includes a spiritual types test (really fun), information
on sacred space and spiritual disciplines, articles, news, and a
bookstore.

Next Wave International, www.nextwaveinternational.com. An international mission to youth and young adults. Gives a global perspective
on today's youth with an emphasis on Europe.

Taizé Community, www.taize.fr. The Web page of the Taizé community
where thousands of young people go for study, prayer, and community. Offers a global perspective on today's youth.

Youth Ministry and Spirituality Project, www.ymsp.com. This organization has done exemplary work in youth ministry, and it helps congregations integrate spirituality with youth ministry. Includes articles,
results of youth ministry projects, a newsletter, and contemplative
spiritual practices.

Youth Specialties, www.youthspecialties.com. Excellent source of information for the spiritual formation of youth and young adults.
Includes articles, links to other resources, bookstore, annual conven-
tion, training opportunities for youth workers.

If you are associated with a particular denomination, consult your own
denominational Web page. Or look at the Web pages of other
denominations.

BOOKS

Dean, Kenda Creasy, and Ron Foster. *The Godbearing Life: The Art of
Soul Tending for Youth Ministry*. Nashville: Upper Room Books,
1998. The book's focus is the need for God in the lives of teens and
youth workers. Includes ways to prepare youth workers, ideas for
youth ministry, suggested questions/exercises, and ways to teach
spiritual practices.

Humphrey, Nathan, ed. *Gathering the Next Generation: Essays on the
Formation and Ministry of GenX Priests*. Harrisburg, PA: Morehouse
Publishing, 2000. While this book is a series of essays for the mentoring of Episcopal priests, the information is easily transferable to
seminarians and serious young adult seekers.

Jones, Tony, et al. *Postmodern Youth Ministry: Exploring Cultural Shift,
Creating Holistic Connections, Cultivating Authentic Community*.
Grand Rapids, MI: Zondervan, 2001. This book is written for youth
workers, and it includes chapters on postmodernism, community,
evangelism, the Bible, the value of story, and ways to use spiritual
practices.

Yaconelli, Mark. *Contemplative Youth Ministry: Practicing the Presence of
Jesus*. Grand Rapids, MI: Zondervan, 2006. The focus of this book is
to help youth workers listen to God so they can minister to young
people.

BIBLIOGRAPHY: RECOMMENDED RESOURCES

PRAYER AND SPIRITUAL PRACTICES
BOOKS

Case, Steven L. *The Book of Uncommon Prayer: Contemplative and Celebratory Prayers and Worship Services for Youth Ministry.* Grand Rapids, MI: Zondervan, 2002. Includes various liturgical services, prayers, responsive readings, and private devotions.

Foster, Richard. *Prayer: Finding the Heart's True Home.* New York: HarperSanFrancisco, 1992. Excellent resource on how to pray. Chapters include "Simple Prayer," "Prayer of Tears," "Prayer of Relinquishment," "Sacramental Prayer," "Unceasing Prayer," "Prayer of Rest," "Contemplative Prayer," Healing Prayer," "Authoritative Prayer," "Radical Prayer."

Greg, Pete, and Dave Roberts. *Red Moon Rising: How 24-7 Prayer Is Awakening a Generation.* Orlando, FL: Relevant Books, 2005. The remarkable story of people devoted to praying on behalf of nations, peoples, and situations.

Jones, Tony. *Soul Shaper: Exploring Spirituality and Contemplative Practices in Youth Ministry.* Grand Rapids, MI: Youth Specialties, 2003. A primer on the history and use of spiritual disciplines such as *lectio divina,* Jesus prayer, examen, Daily Office, silence, centering prayer, spiritual direction, the labyrinth, and pilgrimage. The book includes stories of youth and youth workers using these practices.

Lindbloom, Lois. *Is That You, God?: Cultivating Discernment as a Way of Life.* Available from lalindbloom@earthlink.net. A simple booklet explaining discernment tools. Excellent for youth and young adults.

Linn, Dennis. *Sleeping with Bread: Holding What Gives You Life.* Mahwah, NJ: Paulist Press, 1995. Looks like a children's book, but is an excellent description of the practice of examen.

Merrill, Nan C. *Psalms for Praying: An Invitation to Wholeness.* New York: Continuum, 2002. This work is a softer contemporary paraphrase of the Psalms that appeals to young people.

Peterson, Eugene. *The Message: The New Testament, Psalms, and Proverbs in Contemporary Language.* Colorado Springs: NavPress, 2002.

Sirchino, Bryan, and Joe Steinke. *High Frequency: Words to the Song.*

Minneapolis: Augsburg Fortress, 2001. A short workbook of contemplative prayer practices for youth. Includes ways to use music, *lectio divina*, journaling, discernment, and silence as prayer practices.

Wolpert, Dan. *Creating a Life with God: The Call of Ancient Prayer Practices*. Nashville: Upper Room Books, 2003. A practical explanation of the ancient prayer practices of *lectio divina*, the Jesus prayer, the examen, journaling, body prayer, and communal prayer.

WEB PAGES THAT PROVIDE INSTRUCTION IN VARIOUS SPIRITUAL PRACTICES

Centering Prayer, www.centeringprayer.org. Contemplative Outreach.

Labyrinth, www.grace.org. Grace Cathedral, San Francisco, earliest church in the United States to use the labyrinth.

Labyrinth, www.labyrinth.co.uk.

Lectio divina, www.lectiodivina.org.

Pilgrimage, www.christian-travelers-guides.com.

FAITH AND BELIEFS OF YOUTH AND YOUNG ADULTS

Beliefnet, www.beliefnet.com. A multi-faith community with articles on God, faith, and spirituality. Includes short descriptions of the beliefs of many Christian and non-Christian faith traditions.

Beaudoin, Tom. *Virtual Faith: The Irreverent Spiritual Quest of Generation X*. San Francisco: Jossey-Bass, 1998. One of the earliest works on the faith life of Generation X. Excellent material on popular culture.

Blogs 4 God, www.blogs4god.com. A Web page of Christian blogs on the following categories: apologia, church polity, journals, metablogs, ministries, pundits, techblogs, zines. The blogs are written by people of all ages; however, because of the nature of the technology, young adults seem to do most of the blogging. This is also an excellent way to read about what young people think and an excellent introduction to blogging.

Fashbaugh, Edward M., II. *Creating an Authentic Youth Ministry*. Nashville: Upper Room, 2005. Includes chapters on adult involvement, faith formation, teen empowerment, and personal transformation.

Parks, Sharon Daloz. *Big Questions, Worthy Dreams: Mentoring Young Adults in Their Search for Meaning, Purpose, and Faith.* San Francisco: Jossey-Bass, 2000. Good discussion on the development of the young adult's faith and on mentoring communities.

Schwadel, Paul, and Christian Smith. *Portraits of Protestant Teens: A Report on Teenagers in Major U.S. Denominations.* Oxford, OH: Oxford Press, 2005. A report on the national study (U.S.) of teenagers and faith. Contains facts, statistics, and graphs.

Smith, Christian, and Melinda Lundquist Denton. *The Religious and Spiritual Lives of American Teenagers.* Oxford, OH: Oxford Press, 2005. The focus is the national study on teenagers and faith. Contains facts, statistics, and graphs.

The Taizé Community (Videotape). Ateliers it Presses de Taizé. Distributed in North America by GIA Publications, Chicago.

Tassi, Peter. *The Beauty Within: Inspirational Stories and Practical Advice for Anyone Who Works (or Lives) with Teenagers.* Denver: Living the Good News, 1999.

www.ucla.edu/news. Results of a national (U.S.) study of college students searching for meaning and purpose in life.

Youth and Religion, www.youthandreligion.org. A report on the national study (U.S.) of adolescents and faith. Contains facts, statistics, and graphs.

PSYCHOLOGICAL DEVELOPMENT OF YOUNG PEOPLE

Levine, Mel. *Ready or Not, Here Life Comes.* New York: Simon & Schuster, 2005. The book's focus is on today's twentysomethings and why they are having difficulty becoming adults.

Robbins, Alexandra, and Abby Wilner. *Quarterlife Crisis: The Unique Challenges of Life in Your Twenties.* New York: JP Tarcher/Putnam, 2001. Written by two women in their twenties, this book is an authentic representation of the issues facing today's twentysomethings.

POSTMODERNISM

Ackerman, John. *Listening to God: Spiritual Formation in Congregations.* Herndon, VA: Alban Institute, 2001. This book presents a concrete and practical guide on introducing spiritual formation into churches.

Kitchens, Jim. *The Postmodern Parish: New Ministry for a New Era.* Herndon, VA: Alban Institute, www.alban.org. Discusses the shifts in ministry that have taken place in the postmodern congregation. Focus is on worship, Christian formation, mission, and leadership. Not directly applicable to youth, but it does provide insights into the issues facing the postmodern church.

Sweet, Leonard. *Soultsunami: Sink or Swim in New Millennium Culture.* Grand Rapids, MI: Zondervan, 1999.

THE FOLLOWING WORKS ARE LENGTHY AND ACADEMIC

Carroll, Colleen. *The New Faithful: Why Young Adults Are Embracing Christian Orthodoxy.* Chicago: Loyola Press, 2002.

Ludwig, Robert A. *Reconstructing Catholicism for a New Generation.* New York: Crossroad, 1996. This book revisits doctrines of the Catholic Church and brings them into a postmodern setting.

Webber, Robert E. *Ancient-Future Faith: Rethinking Evangelicalism for a Postmodern World.* North Dartmouth, MA: Baker, 1999. An excellent resource for the evangelical church. Brings the richness of ancient Christian traditions to today's seekers.

SPIRITUAL DIRECTION

Bakke, Jeannette. *Holy Invitations.* North Dartmouth, MA: Baker, 2000. Possibly the best description of the ministry of spiritual direction. Extremely helpful in the preparation of spiritual directors.

Ball, Peter. *Introducing Spiritual Direction.* London: SPCK, 2003. Excellent description of spiritual direction from a British author.

Dougherty, Rose Mary, ed. *The Lived Experience of Group Spiritual Direction.* Mahwah, NJ: Paulist Press, 2003. Includes chapters on doing group direction with teenagers, seminarians, and clergy.

May, Gerald. *Care of Mind, Care of Spirit: A Psychiatrist Explores Spiritual Direction.* New York: HarperCollins, 1992.

Spiritual Directors International, www.sdi.org. This Web site offers information on spiritual direction and on ways to find a spiritual director.

CHRISTIAN HISTORY, TWENTIETH AND TWENTY-FIRST CENTURIES

Cimino, Richard, and Don Lattin. *Shopping for Faith: American Religion in the New Millennium.* San Francisco: Jossey-Bass, 1998. A commentary on religious movements, science, the media, women in ministry, the computer age, and the evangelical megachurches. The authors make insightful observations and predictions.

Foster, Richard. *Streams of Living Water: Celebrating the Great Traditions of Christian Faith.* New York: HarperCollins, 1998. A brief history as well as information about the current practice of traditions of the twentieth- and twenty-first-century church: contemplative tradition, holiness tradition, charismatic tradition, social justice tradition, evangelical tradition, and incarnational tradition.

Holt, Bradley. *Thirsty for God: A Brief History of Christian Spirituality.* Minneapolis: Augsburg Fortress, 2005. A concise history of Christianity since its beginnings to the present day.

Tickle, Phyllis. "Unwrapping Religion," www.explorefaith.com/phyllistickle.

Wuthnow, Robert. *After Heaven: Spirituality in America Since the 1950s.* Los Angeles: University of California Press, 1998. Includes the distinction between dweller and seeker spirituality.

GENERATIONS

Hicks, Rick, and Kathy Hicks. *Boomers, Xers, and Other Strangers: Understanding the Generational Differences that Divide Us.* Carol Stream, IL: Tyndale, 1999.

Strauss, William, and Neil Howe. *American's 13th Generation, Born 1961–1981.* New York: Vintage Books, 1993. Information on today's young adults and those approaching middle age.

———. *Generations: The History of America's Future, 1584–2069.* New York: Vintage Books, 1991. A fascinating theory that the generations in the United States have repeated themselves since the birth of this nation. Commentary on the five generations that exist today. An excellent resource for anyone working with people who are not of your generation.

———. *Millennials Rising: The Next Great Generation.* New York:

Vintage Books, 2000. A wealth of information on the newest generation, those born between 1980 and 2002.

PERSONAL SPIRITUAL ENRICHMENT FOR THOSE WHO COMPANION YOUTH AND YOUNG ADULTS

I hesitate to recommend books to people for personal use. I feel people need to seek the guidance of the Holy Spirit and the help of their spiritual director. However, I can suggest a few books that have helped many people as they have gone through our spiritual direction preparation program. All are on developing a life of prayer, and all are concise and practical.

Beckmen, Richard. *Prayer: Beginning Conversations with God.* Minneapolis: Augsburg Press, 1995. This is an excellent introduction to the many styles of prayer.

Hall, Thelma. *Too Deep for Words: Rediscovering Lectio Divina, With 500 Scripture Texts for Prayer.* Mahwah, NJ: Paulist Press, 1988. For those who want to delve deeper into the spiritual practice of *lectio divina.*

Nesser, Joann. *Journey into Reality: Through Prayer and God-Centeredness.* Vancouver, WA: Living Waters Publishing, 1998. This book focuses on the journey one takes to come into God's presence and the transformation that can happen.

Nouwen, Henri. *The Way of the Heart.* New York: Ballantine, 1981. A classic book on the value of solitude, silence, and prayer.